Collaborative Learning Handbook

Contemporary Marketing
TWELFTH EDITION

Louis E. Boone
University of South Alabama

David L. Kurtz
University of Arkansas

THOMSON
SOUTH-WESTERN

Australia · Canada · Mexico · Singapore · Spain · United Kingdom · United States

THOMSON

SOUTH-WESTERN

Collaborative Learning Handbook to accompany Contemporary Marketing, 12/e

Louis E. Boone & David L. Kurtz

VP/Editorial Director:
Jack W. Calhoun

VP/Editor-in-Chief:
Dave Shaut

Publisher:
Melissa Acuña

Executive Editor:
Neil Marquardt

Developmental Editor:
Rebecca von Gillern

Marketing Manager:
Nicole Moore

Senior Promotions Manager:
Terron Sanders

Production Editor:
Margaret M. Bril

Technology Project Editor:
Kristen Meere

Media Editor:
Karen Schaffer

Manufacturing Coordinator:
Diane Lohman

Printer:
Webcom
Toronto, Ontario

Art Director:
Michelle Kunkler

Cover and Internal Designer:
Liz Harasymczuk Design

Cover Images:
© Getty Images and © Corbis

Photography Manager:
John Hill

Photo Researchers:
Darren Wright and Annette Coolidge

COPYRIGHT © 2006
by South-Western, part of the Thomson Corporation. South-Western, Thomson, and the Thomson logo are trademarks used herein under license.

Printed in Canada
1 2 3 4 5 07 06 05 04

ISBN: 0-324-23683-2

The text of this publication, or any part thereof, may be reproduced for use in classes for which **Contemporary Marketing, 12e** by **Louis E. Boone and David L. Kurtz** is the adopted textbook. It may not be reproduced in any manner whatsoever for any other purpose without written permission from the publisher.

For permission to use material from this text or product, submit a request online at http://www.thomsonrights.com.

For more information contact South-Western,
5191 Natorp Boulevard,
Mason, Ohio 45040.
Or you can visit our Internet site at:
http://www.swlearning.com

Collaborative Learning Handbook

Contemporary Marketing

TWELFTH EDITION

Table of Contents

Chapter 1	Marketing: Creating Satisfaction through Customer Relationships	1
Chapter 2	Strategic Planning and the Marketing Process	9
Chapter 3	The Marketing Environment, Ethics, and Social Responsibility	17
Chapter 4	E-Commerce: Marketing in the Digital Age	23
Chapter 5	Consumer Behavior	31
Chapter 6	Business-to-Business (B2B) Marketing	37
Chapter 7	Serving Global Markets	43
Chapter 8	Managing Marketing Information	51
Chapter 9	Market Segmentation, Targeting, and Positioning	57
Chapter 10	Relationship Marketing, Customer Relationship Management (CRM), and One-to-One Marketing	63
Chapter 11	Product Strategies	69
Chapter 12	Category and Brand Management, Product Identification, and New-Product Planning	77
Chapter 13	Marketing Channels and Supply Chain Management	83
Chapter 14	Direct Marketing and Marketing Resellers: Retailers and Wholesalers	89
Chapter 15	Integrated Marketing Communications	95
Chapter 16	Advertising and Public Relations	101
Chapter 17	Personal Selling and Sales Promotion	107
Chapter 18	Pricing Concepts and Approaches	115
Chapter 19	Pricing Strategies	120

Contemporary Marketing
Collaborative Learning Handbook

While some introductory marketing students are highly prepared and strongly focused, others lack basic skills and reasonable attention spans. But all students—regardless of their background—learn the most when they are fully engaged in the learning experience. The challenge is *how* to hook the interest of students from such varied backgrounds, and still cover the flood of crucial material in any introductory marketing class.

This book is designed to provide you with ideas to bring introductory marketing to life in the classroom. Each interactive exercise is tied (by section name and page number) to specific material in Boone and Kurtz *Contemporary Marketing, 12e*. Based on your needs, you could use them in each class period or sprinkle them occasionally through the term; we encourage you to cherry-pick the ones that would be most effective in your classroom.

Respecting your busy schedule, and your need to cover a huge volume of material, these exercises are short. The goal is to spark student interest in quick bursts that keep them engaged as you lecture on each topic. Virtually all activities use less than 30 minutes of class time, and most use 20 minutes or less. The vast majority of exercises do not require advance preparation or additional materials.

A few comments and suggestions:

- If you don't typically do interactive exercises, warn your students in advance that you'll be trying something new. Get them involved, and ask for their feedback after each exercise…typically they have great ideas that will help you be more effective next time.

- For maximum impact, keep group sizes no greater than 7 and no less than 3. It also helps to switch between allowing students working with their friends and insisting on a more random mix (keep in mind that random mixes tend to take more time).

- The times allocated for each exercise may seem short, but they are completely adequate. When in doubt, call time a bit too early rather than a bit too late. The result will be a significantly higher energy level.

- You may want to keep some inexpensive candy on-hand to provide token prizes for winning individuals or teams (it's amazing how hard some students will work for a Tootsie Roll!)

- Typically, these exercises work well for classes of up to 50 students, although many of them—especially the discussion-based exercises—can be adapted for larger groups.

Chapter 1
Creating Satisfaction through Customer Relationships

Definition of Marketing

Purpose:
　　To introduce marketing in a way that your students will understand on a more personal level

Background:
　　The formal definition of marketing is rather abstract, which makes it somewhat difficult for many students to grasp. This quick, discussion-based exercise helps students understand the impact of marketing on a more concrete, personal level, which should lead to a better understanding of the formal definition.

Relationship to text:
　　What Is Marketing? (page 6)

Estimated Class Time:
　　Less than 10 minutes

Preparation/Materials:
　　None needed

Exercise:
　　Ask your class how many of them ate the last meal (breakfast, lunch, or dinner) depending on the time of your class. Then, call on individual students to share what they ate. Be sure to ask specific questions regarding the marketing mix. For example, why did you choose that cereal? Who bought the bacon and eggs? From what store? Why did you go to Starbucks? Where did you first hear of that pancake house? With your guidance, they will quickly see the impact of product, price, place, and promotion on their day-to-day lives, which will help them internalize the broader meaning of marketing.

Questions for Reflection:
- Beyond the elements of the marketing mix, what factors influence consumer decision-making?
- Do you think the marketing field is ethical? Socially responsible? Why or why not?
- Can not-for-profit organizations benefit from marketing? How?

Not-for-Profit Marketing

Purpose:
    To highlight a key challenge of not-for-profit marketing

Background:
    While nearly 10% of the U.S. workforce either works or volunteers at not-for-profit organizations, many students do not recognize that marketing plays a critically important role at these organizations. This quick, discussion-based exercise is designed to highlight not just the importance of marketing, but also a key difference in marketing not-for-profits: the frequent need to focus on multiple "publics."

Relationship to Text:
    Characteristics of Not-for-Profit Marketing (page 16)

Estimated Class Time:
    About 10 minutes

Preparation/Materials:
    Marker and white board

Exercise:
    NOTE: This exercise is only relevant for non-profit public or private colleges and universities (which compose the vast majority of the higher education market).

    Ask your students to brainstorm the various "publics" that your school targets. Most classes quickly identify students and faculty, but it often takes them a moment to recognize how broad the list can actually be. (The less obvious possibilities include employers, taxpayers, book publishers, the local community, etc.) Write their responses on the board, and then ask them to consider the list: How does their school prioritize those publics? Why? How do they see the results of these decisions? Do they agree or disagree with the school's approach? The student comments are typically interesting and thoughtful. In fact, you may want to ask someone from your school's marketing group to join the discussion, add real-world insights, and benefit from your class' perspective.

Questions for Reflection:
- Why do non-for-profit organizations often need to serve multiple publics?
- Does this characteristic make them more or less effective? Why?

Person Marketing

Purpose:
>To demonstrate the prevalence and power of person marketing in pop culture

Background:
>From athletes, to entertainers, to politicians, person marketing surrounds us all on a continual basis. This exercise is designed to help students understand the various tools and techniques of person marketing, by examining how it can turnaround the image of people in the public eye.

Relationship to Text:
>Person Marketing (page 17)

Estimated Class Time:
>About 15 minutes

Preparation/Materials:
>None needed

Exercise:
>Brainstorm with your class a list of high profile people who need an image makeover (essentially celebrities in trouble). Encourage them to consider athletes, entertainers, and politicians, and to briefly explain why each person needs help. Possibilities include Bobby Brown, Kobe Bryant, Martha Stewart, Janet Jackson, Courtney Love, etc. When you have a list of 10-15 people, discuss with your class the various tools and techniques of people marketing. Possibilities could include everything from straightforward methods such as direct advertising or supporting a high profile charity, to more subtle methods such as creating a distraction (e.g. getting married for the 9th time!!).
>
>Then, divide your students into groups of 5-7 people, and charge each group with rehabilitating the image of the person of their choice. (Keep in mind that this exercise works well even if multiple groups choose the same person.) Five to ten minutes should be enough time.
>
>Reconvene as a class, and ask each group to present its plan, beginning with the objective and following with the strategy. The plans are almost always both instructive and amusing.

Questions for Reflection:
- What are the unique challenges to person marketing?
- Who has done an especially strong job with person marketing? Why?

Place Marketing

Purpose:
>To stimulate student thinking about the potential impact of place marketing

Background:
>Over the past ten years, place marketing has blossomed, as a growing number of cities and states have actively marketed themselves to both businesses and tourists. Among the high profile examples is Las Vegas, which recently introduced a $25 million marketing campaign promoting their racy new slogan: "What Happens Here, Stays Here." This exercise is designed to help students explore the multiple possibilities of place marketing.

Relationship to Text:
>Place Marketing (page 18)

Estimated Class Time:
>About 15-20 minutes

Preparation/Materials:
>None needed

Exercise:
>Divide your class into groups of 5-7, and challenge them to develop a plan to lure businesses and tourists to their city. Questions to consider (and you might want to write these on the board):
>- What would their slogan be?
>- What qualities and attractions would they promote, and why?
>- What challenges would they need to overcome?
>- What companies or organizations might they choose as partners and why?

Encourage your students to push the edge of the envelope in terms of creativity.

>Reconvene as a class for brief presentations of the slogans and the plans. To bolster the competitive spirit, you may want to ask the class to vote on the best package (but don't let any group vote for itself!).

Questions for Reflection:
>- Is place marketing a good way to spend taxpayer dollars? Why or why not?
>- What are some private destinations (e.g. Disney World) that have done especially well at place marketing? What tools have they used?

Creativity

Purpose:
>To emphasize the importance of creativity in marketing (and to have a bit of fun with it!)

Background:
>In today's hyper-competitive marketplace, businesses must differentiate their products and services from the wide range of alternatives. While dynamic innovation is rare (and life-changing), many successful products depend on providing a new twist on an existing product. Examples include Jet Blue's cable-TV-for-every-seat, Apple's translucent, multi-colored computer monitors, and Colgate's pump toothpaste dispenser. This activity is designed to exercise the creativity that is crucial for business innovation.

Relationship to Text:
>Competitive Differentiation (page 11)
>Critical Thinking (page 21)

Estimated Class Time:
>About 10 minutes

Preparation/Materials:
>None needed

Exercise:

Rebus puzzles present common words and phrases in novel orientation to each other. The goal is to determine the meaning. Write each puzzle on the board, and challenge your students to determine the meaning. NOTE: Often one student "gets it" instantly; if so, you may want to ask that person to hold off for a moment to give others a chance. The puzzles (and the answers) are below. If you want to go one step further, you might ask students to create their own rebus puzzles.

ARREST
YOU'RE
(You're under arrest)

abcdefghjmo
pqustuvwxyz
(Missing link)

HISTORY
HISTORY
HISTORY
(History repeats itself)

TimeTime
(Time after time or double time)

Chimadena
(Made in China)

YYYGuy
(Wise guy)

RIGHT   RIGHT
(Equal rights)

scope
(Microscope)

MEREPEAT
(Repeat after me)

XQQQMe
(Excuse me!)

BAN ANA
(Banana split)

BPULSEIANSEUSRSE
(Mixing business with pleasure)

Questions for Reflection:
- How can companies nurture creativity? How can they stifle it?
- How important is creativity to a successful career?
- What are some ways that you could exercise your own creativity?

Chapter 2
Strategic Planning and the Marketing Process

Planning throughout the Organization

Purpose:
　　To highlight a key challenge in gathering information for strategic planning

Background:
　　The research is clear: when your entire organization gathers and shares information, the planning process is more effective and better integrated into the organizational culture. But the best way to achieve full employee participation is much less clear. This exercise is designed to help students explore potential approaches to achieve more widespread information sharing.

Relationship to Text:
　　Planning at Different Organization Levels (page 41)

Estimated Class Time:
　　About 10-15 minutes

Preparation/Materials
　　None needed

Exercise:
　　Ask your class why they think it is so difficult to achieve a free flow of information and ideas in most companies. As they share their thoughts, you may want to point out that money isn't always the answer; in fact, offering money in exchange for ideas can spawn a counterproductive, competitive dynamic among employees at all levels. Ironically, technology doesn't always help either. Joseph Priestley, a pioneer of modern science, summed-up a common issue by observing, "The more elaborate our means of communication, the less we communicate."

　　After a brief discussion, break your class into teams of 5-7 people, and give them about five minutes to brainstorm possible solutions. When you re-convene as a class, ask each group to share their best idea (possibilities usually range from ideas such as hosting weekly planning lunches with all employees, to engaging Intranet approaches, to raising overall pay). This often leads to a helpful, spontaneous discussion of which works better and why.

Questions for Reflection:
- How does planning connect to corporate culture?
- Is employee participation likely to become more or less important as our economy evolves? Why?

Defining the Organization's Mission and Objectives

Purpose:
> To give students a personal perspective on mission statements

Background:
> This exercise is designed to explore and articulate their personal "mission statements." Typically it is both interesting and inspiring, and helps students understand at a more visceral level how organizations use their mission statements to differentiate themselves and to guide their decision-making

Relationship to Text:
> Defining the Organization's Mission and Objectives (page 42)

Estimated Class Time:
> About 10 minutes

Preparation/Materials:
> Each student will need a paper and pencil/pen.

Exercise:
> Ask each student to spend a few moments writing a personal mission statement for his or her life. Try to smile at the groans (!!) and resist the temptation to give too much further direction. After about five minutes, ask for volunteers to share their statements. If no one volunteers, call on people who are articulate in class. The results can be staggering. Discussion is typically spontaneous, but if not, ask them to identify similarities and differences in their statements, especially across gender, age, and nationality/ethnicity. What do their statements say about ethics, values, and locus of control? How do their personal missions influence their actions and decisions on a day-to-day basis? You may want to close by calling their attention to the obvious parallels between personal and organizational missions.

Questions for Reflection:
- What are the characteristics of a strong mission statement? (You may want to precede this question by sharing examples of your own favorite mission statements. Possibilities: Merck, *To preserve and improve human life*; Mary Kay, *To provide unlimited opportunity for women.*)
- You may want to extend the exercise by asking each student to do a personal SWOT analysis, the logical next step in strategic planning.

Strategic Planning

Purpose:
> To give your students hands-on experience with basic strategic planning for a very familiar entity...themselves!

Background:
> Attempting to implement strategic planning, students often struggle to find the balance between an approach that's too narrow and an approach that's too broad. This exercise is designed to help students achieve the right balance by examining their personal strategic plans (and as an added bonus, they will receive some guidance from their peers about their careers!).

Relationship to Text:
> Strategic Planning (page 44)

Estimated Class Time:
> About 15 minutes

Preparation/Materials:
> Each student will need a paper and pencil/pen

Exercise:
> Give your students a couple of minutes to write down the strategic mission for their careers, looking at the five-year horizon. What do they aspire to be doing from a professional standpoint in five years? Collect the papers, shuffle them, and redistribute them to the class.
>
> Ask each student to write a five point strategic plan for the person whose paper he or she received. Each point in the plan should be no more than a sentence or two. Remind the class to ensure that all of their points are specific, measurable, and most importantly, will bring the student closer to the strategic goal.
>
> After about ten minutes, call on a handful of students, and ask them to share the goal and the five-step plan with the class. (It may be helpful to circulate as they work, so you can ensure that you are able to call on the students with the best plans...)

Questions for Reflection:
- Was it easy or hard to write the plan? Why?
- How could a strategic plan help develop your career? Why?
- How does developing a personal strategic plan compare to developing a business strategic plan?

Formulating a Marketing Strategy

Purpose:

To help students explore strategic solutions for a contemporary marketing issue

Background:

Not surprisingly, fast food restaurants are feeling under siege. Study after study this year has highlighted health hazards of rampant obesity in the US. With the ubiquity of low-carb diets, retail sales of french fries—a staple of fast food restaurants—have plummeted, dropping 2.9% in 2001, 3.3% in 2002, and 10% in 2003 (www.whybiotech.com). From a PR perspective, the documentary *Super Size Me* has fanned the flames. This exercise is designed to help students explore potential solutions—and ethical implications—for this strategic challenge from the fast food industry perspective.

Relationship to Text:

Formulating, Implementing, and Monitoring a Marketing Strategy (page 44)

Estimated Class Time:

About 20-25 minutes

Preparation/Materials:

You may want to copy the background and the case situation for each student.

Exercise:

Divide your class into groups of 5-7 students, and share with them the following mini case.

Situation: You and your teammates are partners in the ownership of a medium-sized fast-food chain in the Midwest. You own 41 outlets, most of them in small towns. The mainstay of your menu is hamburgers and french fries, although you also offer a couple of sandwiches, various chips, soft-serve ice cream, and sodas. Your most important customers are men aged 18-34 (they account for about 20% of your customers and about 55% of your sales), but since restaurant options are limited in most of the towns where you operate, you serve customers across a wide demographic range. Sales in the past two years have been dropping at an accelerating rate, so you are now meeting with your partners to discuss potential solutions.

Give your class about 10 minutes to brainstorm options in their small groups. Encourage them to consider all the possibilities, including doing nothing ("This will all blow over..."). Then, direct each group to choose their best option, and to identify the potential risks and benefits (e.g. If they made changes to attract new customers, will they alienate their current core customers?).

Reconvene as a class, and ask each group to report briefly to their peers. Which solution does the class like best? Why? (Questions for reflection, outlined below, are especially helpful for this exercise.)

Questions for Reflection:
- What additional information do you need to formulate the best solution?
- What are the ethical implications of each choice?
- Should your personal perspective play a role in your strategic decision-making? Why or why not? (You may want to preface this question by asking how many of your students eat fast food more than once a week!)

Promotional Strategy and Pricing Strategy

Purpose:
> To explore the relationship between the promotional and pricing strategies

Background:
> Clearly, all elements of the marketing mix are interrelated. This exercise is designed to highlight the links between promotion and pricing.

Relationship to Text:
> Promotional Strategy and Pricing Strategy (page 51)

Estimated Class Time:
> About 15 minutes

Preparation/Materials:
> Each student needs to have unlined paper and pencil/pen.

Exercise*:
> Break your class into groups of 5 –7 students. Ask each group to choose a good or a service that they all know and like, and to create two ads for that product: one that focuses on price, the other on the features and benefits of the product itself. (They can do print, radio, or TV ads, so long as both use the same media.) Let them know upfront that they'll need to present their ads to the class.
>
> When the teams present their ads, conduct a quick vote of which ad the class liked better for each product. Keeping a tally on the board of the products and the winning type of ad is helpful. Results will vary significantly based on the product categories (and, of course, the creativity of the students!).
>
> Follow-up discussion can be interesting, surprising, and fun. What type of ads worked best, and why? How did the product category and price affect the promotional strategy? Does the broader market reflect the findings of the class? Why or why not?

Questions for Reflection:
- What factors should a company consider when developing their pricing strategies? Their promotional strategies? Why?

---

*This exercise was adapted from the text.

The Marketing Environment

Purpose:
    To highlight the importance of the marketing environment

Background:
    This quick, discussion-based exercise is designed to help students better understand the impact of the external environment on marketing decisions.

Relationship to Text:
    The Marketing Environment (page 51 & 52)

Estimated Class Time:
    About 10 minutes

Materials/Preparation:
    None needed

Exercise:
    Choose a branded product that your students seem to all know and enjoy. Higher-end products, such as an Apple i-Pod or a Burton snowboard seem to work especially well for this exercise.

    Guide your students in a discussion of how each element of the external environment—competitive, political-legal, economic, technological, and social-cultural—could influence the success of their product over the next five years. Encourage them to consider factors beyond the obvious (e.g. the emerging development of year-round snow-makers, or virtual reality snowboarding games). As you develop your list, you may want to also remind them that a marketer cannot control the external environment, but he or she must respond to it effectively.

Questions for Reflection:
- Which element of the marketing environment is most important? Why? Would the answer be different for different product categories?
- Which elements have the most impact on a marketer's day-to-day decision-making? Which elements are likely to generate surprises? (You may want to point out how many companies were surprised by the bursting of the Internet bubble!)
- What are effective ways to monitor the environment on an on-going basis?

BCG Matrix

Purpose:
To help students gain a fuller understanding of the BCG matrix as a planning tool

Background:
While the concept of the BCG matrix is straightforward, many students have trouble understanding how it applies to actual situations as an investment tool. This exercise is designed to foster a deeper understanding through a hands-on case study approach.

Relationship to Text:
BCG Matrix (page 55)

Estimated Class Time:
About 25 minutes

Materials/Preparation:
None needed

Exercise:
Announce to your class that they will do a case study on the talent agency business (which most of them find more glamorous and exciting than it really is!). Begin by brainstorming a list of movie stars; encourage the class to include a wide variety, from current box office draws, to over-the-hill talents, to emerging stars.

Then, divide your students into groups of 5-7 people, and tell them that each group represents a small talent agency. Their roster includes the stars that you listed on the board.

Give them each ten million hypothetical dollars to invest in marketing the personalities in their stable of stars, and direct them to use the BCG Matrix to make their investment choices. Ask each group to present their allocation and rationale in terms of the matrix. You will probably find that they are tempted to invest big dollars in their "cash cows," which makes for an interesting follow-up discussion.

Questions for Reflection:
- What are the strengths and weaknesses of the BCG Matrix as a strategic planning tool?
- What kind of information do you need to use this tool most effectively?

Chapter 3
The Marketing Environment, Ethics, and Social Responsibility

Types of Competition

Purpose:
   To help students better understand different sources of competition

Background:
   The ability to understand and identify direct and indirect competition can give students a key competitive advantage in the job market. This exercise is designed to help them develop that skill (and to have some fun at the same time!)

Relationship to Text:
   Types of Competition (page 80)

Estimated Class Time:
   About 10 minutes

Preparation/Materials:
   None needed

Exercise:
   Divide your students into teams of 3-5 students. Challenge the teams to brainstorm examples of direct and indirect competition…with a two-minute time limit on each category!

   After you call time, ask one person from each group to bring the lists to the front and read them aloud in turn. Here is the key rule: If more than one group has an example, everyone needs to cross that example from the lists. (You may find that you have to referee whether or not certain examples are legitimate.)

   After several moments, each group will have a unique list of examples. The winner in each category, of course, is the team with the longest remaining list. A few extra credit points for the winning teams will usually make the competition more engaging for everyone.

Questions for Reflection:
- Why does the source of competition matter?
- What are the risks of underestimating indirect competition? What companies (or industries) have been causalities of indirect competitors?

Government Regulation

Purpose:
>To provide context for the current debate regarding whether or not the Internet should be regulated

Background:
>Both state and federal regulators are currently investigating ways to control e-fraud and other ethical issues on the Web. With so many students on the Internet for both business and pleasure, they typically provide a wealth of information about how the Web can be used in ethically shaky ways. This brief, discussion-based exercise is designed to use that knowledge as a springboard to highlight key ethical issues.

Relationship to Text:
>Government Regulation (page 84) NOTE: This also works with Ethical Issues in Marketing (page 97)

Estimated Class Time:
>About 10 minutes

Preparation/Materials:
>None needed

Exercise:
>Ask your students to brainstorm specific ways that the Web could be used for e-commerce in a fraudulent or unethical way. You may be surprised (possibly even shocked!) at what they come up with. One example: searching for misspelled entries on E-Bay (e.g. Playstation listed mistakenly as Raystation), buying at rock-bottom prices and immediately selling for top dollar. Recognizing how easy it could be to cheat others, many Internet savvy students have become increasingly wary about buying and selling on-line.
>
>Discussion Questions: Does your class believe that Internet security is getting better or worse? How many feel uncomfortable sharing personal information (and credit card information) online? What precautions would make them feel more comfortable? How could businesses best reassure their customers? Finally, what role should government play in regulating the Web?

Questions for Reflection:
> - Given that the Internet is global, who should be responsible for policing fraud? Why?
> - How does online shopping compare to "on-ground" shopping in terms of security? Why?

The Economic and Social Cultural Environments

Purpose:

To highlight the role of trust in the external marketing environment

Background:

A recent *Newsweek* article pointed out that the level of trust within a culture correlates strongly with national economic health: the higher the trust, the stronger the economy. One reason may be that with more trust people are more willing to invest and save, and quicker to work with others. * This exercise, taken from a description in the article, is designed to vividly demonstrate the level of trust between individuals, and the economic benefits of a higher level of trust.

Relationship to Text:

The Economic Environment (page 89) and The Social Cultural Environment (page 95)

Estimated Class Time:

About 15 minutes

Preparation/Materials:

Try to get your hands on about $1,000 in play money of various denominations (*Monopoly* money works great). Even without play money, the game is effective, but you will definitely need a whiteboard and at least three markers.

Exercise:

Introduce this exercise as a way to learn more about the role of trust in the economic and social environments. Then, ask for nine volunteers to come to the front of the room. Be sure to choose both passive and assertive people, both men and women. Divide the volunteers into three groups of three, and ask each group to appoint person *A, B,* and *C*. Then explain the game:

The objective of the game is for each person to earn as much money as possible. Persons *A* and *B* are players, and Person *C* is a mediator. The game has ten rounds.
- In each round, Person *A* begins with $10. He can invest that $10 with Person *B*, or keep it.
- If Person *A* chooses to invest with Person *B*, then Person *B* will receive triple the money.
- Person *B* can either keep the money, or return any portion of it to Person *A*.
- The job of Person *C* is to keep track—using the whiteboard—of who has how much money at the end of each round (if you are using play money, person *C* actually awards the dollars).

Before you begin the game, give each player a moment or two to develop a strategy. When the tenth round is finished, ask the Cs to tally the results and report to the class. As you lead a discussion on the winners and losers, be sure your class understands that trusting your partner generates stronger results for both of you. If A kept all the money, B would have nothing, but A would never go above $10 per round. If B didn't return more than $10, A would stop investing. In fact, A would probably stop investing if B returned less than half of the money, because A would feel betrayed.

Follow-up discussion is usually rich and spontaneous. Who earned the most money? Why? How hard was it to trust your partner? Were there differences between men and women?

Questions for Reflection:
- How does trust on a societal level relate to a stronger economy?
- How can governments encourage (or discourage) trust?
- Is trust in general growing or declining in current US culture?
- If you have international students, you may want to ask how their home cultures compare to American culture.

* Source: Adler, Jerry, "Mind Reading," *Newsweek*, July 5th, 2004

Ethics and Legality

Purpose:
To clarify the difference between ethical and legal behavior

Background:
Many students have never thought about laws as the "floor" for ethical behavior; some, in fact, regard laws as the standard rather than the base. This issue is especially important from a marketing perspective, since marketing activities often affect the public far beyond the organization itself. This exercise is designed to clarify the difference between legal and ethical approaches, and in doing so, to help students articulate their own personal ethical standards.

Relationship to Text:
Ethical Issues in Marketing (page 97)

Estimated Class Time:
About 10 minutes

Preparation/Materials:
None needed

Exercise:
Ask your class to identify examples of the following behaviors. You might find it helpful to present the categories on the board as quadrants, and to fill each quadrant with the examples that your students surface.
- Illegal and unethical behavior (e.g. embezzling money, price discrimination, sexual harassment)
- Illegal and ethical behavior (e.g. providing rock-bottom prices only to struggling wholesalers in an underserved rural area)
- Legal and unethical behavior (e.g. promoting R-rated movies to young teens, engaging in employee favoritism)
- Legal and ethical behavior (e.g. leading by example, contributing to the local community, protecting whistleblowers)

You may find that simply categorizing behaviors triggers a vibrant discussion.

Questions for Reflection:
- What tools could companies use to ensure that they market in an ethical manner?
- How involved should the government be in this arena? Are there limits to the effectiveness of regulation?
- What are examples of self-regulation (e.g. the movie rating system, alcohol advertising limits in network TV)? How effective are these efforts? Why?

Ethics and Profits

Purpose:
> To explore the relationship between ethics and profits

Background:
> William Clay Ford, Jr., CEO of Ford, recently said, "There's no incompatibility between doing the right thing and making money" (page ___ of text). While virtually all students would agree, some question whether they could make even more money by stretching ethical limits. This exercise is designed to help students develop their personal ethical perspective by exploring these boundaries.

Relationship to Text:
> Ethical Issues in Marketing (page 97)

Estimated Class Time:
> About 10 minutes

Preparation/Materials:
> None needed

Exercise:
> Ask your students if they believe that ethical behavior leads to higher profits. Most classes respond with a resounding "yes!" But regardless of their responses, share with them the story of the Vice Fund. This is a mutual fund, launched toward the end of 2002, which specializes in "vice" stocks: gambling, defense, alcohol, and tobacco. In the five years prior to launch, Vice Fund stocks went up 53%, while the S&P 500 went up 12%, and the Domini index of socially responsible companies went up 5%. Some argued that this was the result of a economy in recession, but even in the stronger economy of 2003, the Vice Fund went up 34%, while the S&P 500 and the Domini index both increased by 28%.
>
> How do your students respond to this information? Guide them in a discussion of reasons for ethical decision-making that go beyond profitability. Are ethics different from person-to-person? How does this impact decision-making? Most classes conclude that the most important consideration is for each person to act—within the law—according to his or her own values. They quickly understand that the best way to make this happen is to completely understand their own values, both right now, and as they evolve.

Questions for Reflection:
> - How would you react if your values were different from your boss' values? When is this most likely to be an issue for you personally?
> - How would you feel about marketing a product that you don't believe in?

Sources: Maranjian, Selena, "Good vs. Evil Mutual Funds," posted May 11, 2004, *The Motley Fool*, www.fool.com; Harris, Dan, "Vice is Nice," posted October 7, 2002, www.abcnews.com

Chapter 4
E-Commerce: Marketing in the Digital Age

Information and the Internet: Urban Legends

Purpose:
> To help students recognize urban legends and understand the importance of checking the facts

Background:
> College students are surprisingly gullible with regard to urban legends, especially given their heavy use of email for daily communication. While most urban legends are harmless, many can cause significant harm to businesses that are targeted by them. (They can also deeply undermine the credibility of those who forward them...) This exercise is designed to highlight the impact of urban legends, and to underscore the importance of recognizing and disregarding them.

Relationship to Text:
> Four Web Functions: Information (page 123)

Estimated Class Time:
> About 10 minutes

Preparation/Materials:
> Each student will need paper and pencil/pen

Exercise:
> Ask your students to number their papers from 1-10, and give them the urban legends quiz below: Which are true and which are false?

> 1. Burma-Shave once promised to send a contest winner to Mars as part of a promotional campaign. (True) http://www.snopes.com/business/market/market.asp

> 2. Coca-Cola used to contain cocaine (True)
> http://www.snopes.com/cokelore/cokelore.asp

> 3. Coca-Cola is an effective spermicide (False)
> http://www.snopes.com/cokelore/cokelore.asp

> 4. The CEO of Procter & Gamble donates a portion of the company's profits to the Church of Satan. (False) http://www.snopes.com/business/alliance/alliance.asp

> 5. Domino's Pizza supports Operation Rescue, an anti-abortion group.) (False)
> http://www.snopes.com/business/alliance/alliance.asp

6. Cups and burger wrappings at In-N-Out Burger are marked with Bible citations. (True) http://www.snopes.com/business/alliance/alliance.asp

7. The Gap takes its name from the gay pride slogan "Gay and Proud" (False) http://www.snopes.com/business/names/names.htm

8. A customer withdraws his million-dollar account from his bank after a bank employee refuses to validate a 50¢ parking stub. (True…The Bank was Old National Band, now part of U.S. Bank) http://www.snopes.com/business/bank/bank.asp

9. Coleco sends death certificates to children who return damaged Cabbage Patch dolls. (False) http://www.snopes.com/business/consumer/consumer.asp

10. Neiman-Marcus charged a customer $250 for their cookie recipe. (False) http://www.snopes.com/business/consumer/consumer.asp

(All of these urban legends are taken from Snopes.com. If you have Web projection capability, you may want to click on each of the specific sites for the interesting—and often very funny—back-story.)

Ask your students to score their quizzes, and share results—which will probably vary wildly—with the rest of the class via a show of hands. Follow-up discussion: What is the impact of these urban legends on the targeted companies? What can they do to combat them? Should they do anything?

Questions for Reflection:
- On a more personal level, what can each student do to determine the veracity of this kind of email? (Possibilities include a quick check on www.snopes.com or http://hoaxbusters.ciac.org. Simply considering the source is often enough as well.)
- What are the ethical implications of forwarding such email without checking?

Language Differences in Online Marketing

Purpose: To demonstrate the importance of multilingualism in e-commerce

Background:
While English is commonly known as the language of business, companies that operate in multiple languages—especially on the Internet—enjoy a growing competitive advantage. This quick, discussion-based exercise is designed to highlight the importance of multilingualism AND to spur students to study at least one additional language to hone their personal competitive edge.

Relationship to Text: Online Marketing Is International Marketing (page 134)

Estimated Class Time: About 5-10 minutes

Preparation/Materials: None needed

Exercise:
Ask your class how many students are fluent in *at least* one language other than English. Ask them to lower their hands if they speak *only* one other language…*only two* other languages, etc. (In some parts of the country, it is common to have at least one student who is fluent in five languages.)

Share with your students this eye-opening information: A survey posted by Global Reach (http://global-reach.biz/blobstats/index.php3) reports that as of March 2004, only 36.8% of the world's Web users are native English speakers (and experts project that number will continue to fall for at least the next ten years, probably longer). Furthermore, *Time* magazine projects that by 2010, native Chinese speakers alone will outnumber English speakers on the web by 17MM people (Source: *Time Global Business*, November 2001).

Why does this matter, given that many consider English to be the "language of business worldwide"? While growing numbers of people do indeed speak English, the research is clear that consumers are four times more likely to buy a product on the Internet if the Website is in their preferred language. This suggests that a multi-lingual approach to Web marketing could have a powerful, positive impact on the bottom line (Sources: Interworld Translations, www.interworldtranslations.com, and *Time Global Business*, November 2001).

If you have students who are non-native English speakers, ask them to comment. Do they prefer shopping in their native language? Why? Which sites are easiest for them to navigate? Are there unsettling differences in color or icons? (One common—and very interesting—response to these questions is that they lack confidence in their understanding of the fine print when they shop in a non-native language.)

Questions for Reflection:
- With a limited budget, which countries should you target first? Why? How would your product category affect this decision?
- Would it make sense for you to learn another language? Which one? Why?

Online Sellers

Purpose:
To explore the brand-building potential of the Internet

Background:
While the range of product availability online has expanded dramatically in the last couple of years, e-commerce does not currently make financial sense for a number of product categories. This exercise is designed to explore how marketers can use the Web to build their brands without including the e-commerce option.

Relationship to Text:
Online Sellers (page 138)

Estimated Class Time:
About 10-15 minutes

Preparation/Materials:
None needed

Exercise:
Brainstorm with your students a list of products that they believe are fundamentally inappropriate for e-commerce. Convenience products (e.g. mustard, pet food, diapers) and experiential products (e.g. a rock-climbing gym, a massage) typically dominate the list.

Break your students into groups of 3-5 people, and ask each group to choose three of the products on the list. How could each company use the Web to build its brand? What objective, strategies, and tactics would make the most sense? How should the Web site look?

Reconvene as a class, and ask each group to share their ideas for one of the products. (You will probably get some duplicate products, which usually sparks an interesting discussion as they compare and contrast strategies.)

Questions for Reflection:
- Should every company invest in a Web site? Why or why not?
- What are examples of strong non-e-commerce sites on the web? (If you have Web projection capability, you may want to take your class on a quick tour of excellent brand-building sites. Possibilities include the Kraft foods site at www.kraftfoods.com, featuring everything from recipes, to coupons, to contests. Another option is the Virgin Cola site at www.virgindrinks.com, with games, downloads, polls, and fun links.)

Online Communities

Purpose:
To demonstrate the importance of creating and managing Web communities

Background:
Creating an active Web community can give a significant competitive edge to virtually any Web business (E-Bay has done this especially well). But understanding the meaning of Web community—the interaction of your customers with each other and with you (the producer) regarding your product or service—can be challenging. This exercise is designed to work through that challenge by giving students the opportunity to create hypothetical communities for a range of different business types.

Relationship to Text:
Online Communities (page 140)

Estimated Class Time:
About 15 minutes

Preparation/Materials:
Develop a list of business types for your students to analyze in small groups. This project is most effective with a broad mix of businesses that would clearly use the Web in different ways. Possibilities include: A guitar shop, a day spa, a car insurance company, a university, a cell phone provider, an ice cream parlor, a vintage clothier, a pet shop, etc.

Exercise:
Divide the class into groups of 3-5 and assign a different business type to each group. Ask the groups to consider what community could mean for their Web site, and to develop a strategy to create an active community. Remind them to be creative. (A pet store site, for example, could sponsor an information exchange for lost animals; an ice cream store site could sponsor a contest to name a new sundae.) As each group presents to the class, encourage constructive discussion. What are the strengths of each approach? How could each be improved?

After the groups have presented, reconvene as a class to discuss. Why does community add value even when it doesn't directly create sales? Help your students see that not being able to control the information flow can be both an opportunity AND a threat, depending on how the business uses the medium. How can they ensure that it becomes an opportunity?

Questions for Reflection:
- Can a community section of a Web site be used for marketing research? How?
- Who has participated in a Web community (e.g. chat rooms, message boards, E-Bay seller reviews)? What worked well? What would improve the experience?

Designing a "Sticky" Web Site

Purpose: To highlight tools that will help build more effective Web sites

Background: A successful Web site depends to a large extent on current, meaningful content, clear, easy navigation, and excellent search capability. But beyond those fundamentals, site enhancements—or stickiness tools—can make a significant difference in the amount of time a surfer will spend on a given site. This exercise is designed to give students a framework for developing relevant features.

Relationship to Text: Building an Effective Web Site (page 143)

Estimated Class Time: About 15 minutes

Preparation/Materials: None needed

Exercise: Ask your students what Web sites they surf most often (and you may need to remind them that you only want to hear about the clean ones!). Why? What sites do they bookmark? Why? Most classes quickly uncover the core issues of a great site (content, navigation, search), but guide them to also consider the compelling extra features. Possibilities include competitions, calculators (mortgage values, sizing), customized shopping guides, news headlines, daily puzzles, stock tickers, video demonstrations, games, cartoons, and quotations.

Once you have a strong list, divide your class into groups of 3-5 students. Ask each group what specific features would grab attention and add value for the Web sites of the following businesses. Encourage them to be innovative…but relevant. You may want to throw out a couple of examples to spark their thinking (e.g. a college bookstore might include a virtual "study break" link on their site, leading to online pool tables).

- A small law firm
- An acupuncture clinic
- A local board sports store (skateboarding, snowboarding, surfing)
- A specialty wine store
- A trendy clothing boutique
- A college bookstore
- A national weekly news magazine site
- A large department store

Ask each group to share their five favorite ideas with the class (and usually their ideas are very creative!).

Questions for Reflection:
- How have Web sites changed over the past five years? How will they change in the future? Why?
- Is Web surfing replacing other activities in people's lives? Does this provide a threat to any other businesses (e.g. television)? How should they respond?

E-Commerce

Purpose:
To help students understand how to increase e-marketing effectiveness

Background:
Sometimes students find it easier to understand e-marketing strategies by examining those that *don't* work rather than those that do. The exercise is designed to help students uncover opportunities to improve the effectiveness of e-marketing for a product or service that they currently do not seek on the Web.

Relationship to Text:
E-Commerce (page 117)

Estimated Class Time:
About 20 minutes

Preparation/Materials:
None needed

Exercise:
Divide your students into groups of 3-5, and ask each group to choose a product or service that most or all of them would NOT currently purchase via the Web. Give them about ten minutes to answer the following questions:
- Why wouldn't they purchase this product or service on the Web?
- How could they make this product or service more appealing on the Web?
- How could they provide added value (without busting the budget)?
- How could they improve customer service and satisfaction?

Ask each group to share their product and their marketing ideas with the class. Encourage them to recognize the huge opportunities yet to be tapped in B2C e-commerce.

Questions for Reflection:
- What B2B products could be better marketed on the Web?
- What are the career opportunities that stem from this potential?

Chapter 5
Consumer Behavior

Ice Cream and Your Personality

Purpose:
To introduce consumer behavior

Background:
As a broad subject that draws from multiple disciplines, consumer behavior can seem impenetrable to some students. This exercise is designed to introduce the topic in a fun, personal way, setting the tone for the rest of the chapter.

Relationship to Text:
Chapter Overview (page 158)

Estimated Class Time:
Less than 10 minutes

Preparation/Materials:
None needed

Exercise:
Several years ago, Edy's Grand Ice Cream, a national manufacturer of ice cream, commissioned a study to determine how ice cream flavor preferences relate to personality. The study, conducted by Dr. Alan Hirsch, Neurological Director of the Smell and Taste Treatment and Research Foundation in Chicago, determined that distinct personality traits correspond with a preference for certain ice cream flavors.

Is this for real??? Yes! The researchers examined personality profiles for a significant cross-section of people, and correlated the results with each person's ice cream flavor preference.

Just for fun, ask your students to choose their favorite flavor of the following options: vanilla, chocolate, butter pecan, banana, strawberry, and chocolate chip. Ask for a show of hands regarding how many prefer each flavor, and write the results on the board. Then share the following summarized profiles:

- Vanilla: You are a flamboyant, impulsive, risk-taker, with close family relationships
- Chocolate: You are lively and flirtatious…the life of the party…but you do get easily bored
- Butter Pecan: You are a take-charge perfectionist with very high standards and strong integrity
- Banana: You are kind, empathetic, and understanding, generous, and easy-going…an excellent spouse or parent

- <u>Strawberry</u>: You are shy, skeptical, and detail-oriented, and you tend to be pessimistic
- <u>Chocolate Chip</u>: You are success-driven, competitive, and achievement oriented, but also generous and charming

Interestingly, when Edy's published their "flavorology" report, they gave the personality profiles a more positive spin, leaving out potentially problematic descriptions, such as pessimistic, and flirtatious. A company spokesperson explained: "We are in the ice cream business to make people happy. This is supposed to be fun, not upsetting."

Also, Dr. Hirsch noted that while the correlations were scientifically reliable, he could not account for the reasons behind them. So…switching favorite flavors won't change your personality!

Questions for Discussion:

- How could a marketer capitalize on a link between personality and product preference?
- Do you think this type of research is a worthwhile investment? Why or why not?

Sources: Wolf, Buck, "You Are What You Eat for Dessert," ABC News, www.abcnews.go.com/sections/us/DailyNews/wolffiles14, accessed 7/10/04; "You Are Your Ice Cream, ABC News, www.abcnews.go.com/sections/GMA/GoodMorningAmerica/GMA010705, accessed 7/10/04; "The Ice Cream Flavor Personality and Compatibility Test," www.angelfire.com/ga/sweetgeorgiapeach/icecream.html, accessed 7/10/04

Cultural Values and Consumer Behavior

Purpose:
> To help students explore their perceptions of U.S. cultural values

Background:
> Culture clearly influences consumer behavior in both obvious and subtle ways, but students need to understand the elements of culture in order to appreciate the true impact of culture. This exercise is designed to help students focus on their perceptions of core values in U.S. culture.

Relationship to Text:
> Core Values in U.S. Culture (page 159)

Estimated Class Time:
> About 10 minutes

Preparation/Materials:
> Whiteboard and marker

Exercise:
> Spend a few moments reviewing with your class the idea of core values. Once they fully understand the concept, divide your students into groups of 5-7 people, and give each group a few minutes to quickly brainstorm a list of core values in U.S. culture (and tell them to base their list on their perceptions, not to copy from the book!). When their lists are complete, ask them to prioritize from most to least important.
>
> Then, reconvene as a class, and ask a representative from each group to share each list. As the volunteers read the values, determine (via a show of hands) whether or not all the other groups include each item, and track the results on the board in two categories: values that all groups have included, and values that one or more groups have excluded (this may cause a bit of confusion…make sure the volunteer has an eraser at the ready!).
>
> Looking at the list will spark an interesting discussion. What values seem to be universal (at least among the small sample size)? Why isn't there more complete agreement among the groups? Most classes will quickly determine that subculture, age, life experience, and social class all play a role in the differing perceptions.

Questions for Reflection:
- Why is it important to explore the core values of national culture?
- How does this information impact marketing?

Opinion Leaders and Consumer Behavior

Purpose:
> To highlight the importance of opinion leaders in consumer behavior

Background:
> The emerging world of blogs has offered a new opportunity for opinion leaders in a wide range of areas to share their information, thoughts, and (of course!) opinions on every issue imaginable. This discussion-based exercise is designed to underscore the marketing implications and the accompanying ethical issues.

Relationship to Text:
> Opinion Leaders (page 164)

Estimated Class Time:
> About 10 minutes

Preparation/Materials:
> None needed

Exercise:
> Depending on your class, you may want to begin by defining blogs: The word is a shortened form of "Web logs"…essentially web diaries, typically hosted by opinionated individuals with intense interest in a narrow topic. Over the past two years, blogs have exploded in terms of influence and popularity with mainstream America. Do any of your students read blogs. Which ones? Why?
>
> Next, share with your class the interesting story of Raging Cow. In early 2003, Dr. Pepper/7Up began rolling out Raging Cow, a new flavored milk product. Part of their strategy was to create a blog, written (ostensibly) by the Cow herself. But more importantly, Dr. Pepper/7Up hired a team of teenage bloggers to promote the product as stealth marketers. Their job was to promote the product—undercover—in their own blogs. The publicity backlash against this tactic (also used by other companies such as Nokia) has been intense.
>
> What does your class think? Why are marketers using this tactic? Is this smart marketing, or is it sleazy? Does it undermine the integrity of the Web? Does it make them think differently about "innocent" postings in their own Web communities? Is there a better way to use blogs for marketing? The discussion potential on this topic is rich.

Questions for Reflection:
- What are other ways that marketers can identify and convert opinion leaders?
- Do opinion leaders matter more in some categories than others? Why?

Sources: Grossman, Lev, "Meet Joe Blog," *Time*, June 21, 2004; Walker, Rob, "Blogging for Milk," *Slate Magazine*, www.slate.com, April 14th, 2003

Attitudes and Consumer Behavior

Purpose:
To emphasize the role of attitudes in consumer behavior

Background:
While everyone knows what it means to "have an attitude," the marketing implications are less apparent for many students. This exercise is designed to clarity the relationship between attitudes and consumer behavior.

Relationship to Text:
Attitudes (page 171)

Estimated Class Time:
About 20 minutes

Preparation/Materials:
Students will need blank paper, pens/pencils (or ideally colored markers).

Exercise:
Remind your class of the three components of attitude: cognitive, affective, and behavioral. Then, break your students into groups of 3-5 people. Challenge each group to develop three one-page print ads promoting bubble gum, each ad appealing to a different component of attitude (headline and visual are usually sufficient). After ten minutes ask the groups to present their ads to the class. (The results are typically terrific.) When the presentations are complete, ask the class to vote on which appeal was the most effective in marketing bubble gum. Why? What role did the creative itself play in their responses (vs. the type of appeal)?

Questions for Reflection:
- How important are attitudes relative to the other influences on consumer behavior?
- How easy or hard is it to change consumer attitudes? Why? What are the best tools for effecting change?

Self-Concept and Consumer Behavior

Purpose:
To illustrate the close links between whom we are and how we consume

Background:
The study of consumer behavior suggests that many of our purchases reflect recognizable elements of who we are in terms of gender, personality, individual style, hobbies, etc. This exercise is designed to highlight those links.

Relationship to Text:
Self-Concept (page 174)

Estimated Class Time:
About 10 minutes

Preparation/Materials:
Each student will need paper and pen/pencil.

Exercise:
Direct your students to think for a moment about goods or services that they particularly enjoy in any category from shoes, to bands, to cars, to restaurants. Ask them to write down their five favorites, including the brand name (e.g. Nike running shoes, Lucky brand blue jeans), but not to write their own names.

Collect the papers, leaf through them, and choose 5-7 papers that include an assortment of high profile brands. Read the papers aloud to your class, and after each one, ask your class to describe the student who wrote it. (You may want to warn the students in advance not to identify themselves until the rest of the class has a chance to guess.) Usually the writers of the papers choose to identify themselves, and—with some notable exceptions—the profiles guessed by the class, based on the product choices, are astonishingly accurate.

Follow-up discussion is often spontaneous, but if not, you may want to ask how marketers can capitalize on the links between whom people are and what they choose to purchase.

Questions for Reflection:
- In what categories are our purchases most likely to reflect our personalities?
- Do brands themselves have personalities? How can a marketer create a personality for a brand? What is the value in doing so?

Chapter 6
Business-to-Business Marketing

The Business-to-Business Market

Purpose:
> To underscore the similarities and differences between the B2B and the B2C markets

Background:
> While the business-to-business market encompasses a huge percent of our economy, it is largely invisible to many students. This quick brainstorming exercise is designed to highlight the B2B market by comparing it to the B2C market.

Relationship to Text:
> Nature of the Business Market (page 188)

Estimated Class Time:
> About 10 minutes

Preparation/Materials:
> None needed

Exercise:
> Ask your students to brainstorm products that are purchased by both organizations and individuals. Encourage them to stretch. What businesses would buy prepared food? Clothing? Washing machines? For what reasons? What individuals would buy bricks? Lumber? Machines? For what reasons? When you have filled the board with examples, guide them through a discussion: Do the products meet different needs in the business market? Would business customers evaluate the same products according to different criteria? Why? How? This exercise typically serves as a nice introduction to the chapter, since it spurs student thinking about key topics in the B2B market.

Questions for Reflection:
- What are the career opportunities in the B2B market? What are the skills that you would need to succeed in this environment?

Business-to-Business Marketing Strategy

Purpose:
>To provide a hands-on opportunity to consider B2B marketing strategy

Background:
>Successful B2B marketing relies on an effective strategy, which in turn depends on fully understanding the market overall, the target customers, and the strategic options. This exercise—which works best after you cover the key points in the chapter—is designed to help students apply material than can initially seem somewhat abstract.

Relationship to Text:
>Characteristics of the B2B Market (page 194)

Estimated Class Time: About 20 minutes

Preparation/Materials: You may want to copy the scenario and goals (below) for each student.

Exercise:
>After you have covered the characteristics of the B2B market, divide your students into groups of 5-7 people for a brief case study exercise.

>Scenario:
>You and your team were just hired as strategic marketing consultants for a small company that specializes in Web site translation. The company, which is two years old, translates and localizes Websites for organizations with an international presence. They specialize in Spanish, German, Japanese, and Mandarin. The company has done excellent work for a handful of low profile, medium-sized businesses: a wood furniture wholesaler, a trendy clothing retailer, and a plastic molding producer. The company would like to expand their business, which is where you come into play.

>Goals:
>In the next 10-15 minutes, you and your team will develop a concise strategic overview to prepare for an upcoming lunch with the CEO of the company. You must briefly address the following issues: How would you segment the market? Who would you target? Why? How would you approach the market? Write a discussion outline, including a brief description of your target, and a five step marketing strategy (a sentence or two per step). Be sure to clarify any assumptions that you make along the way.

>When the teams have completed their outlines, ask each group to present to the class. You may be surprised at the diversity and creativity of their approaches.

Questions for Reflection:
> - What kind of information would you need to do an actual strategic marketing plan?
> - In general, how does B2B strategy differ from B2C strategy?

Buying versus Making

Purpose:
To examine the key considerations behind a decision to buy component parts versus producing them internally

Background:
A huge number of products contain multiple components purchased from outside suppliers. This exercise is designed to explore the issues that manufacturers consider in making those purchase decisions, plus the related marketing implications.

Relationship to Text:
Make, Buy, or Lease (page 199)

Estimated Class Time:
About 10 minutes

Preparation/Materials:
None needed

Exercise:
Divide your class into groups of 3-5 students, and ask each group to ensure that at least one member has a backpack. Instruct the groups to examine the backpack. What elements compose the product (zippers, handles, etc.)? Which do they think were purchased, and which were manufactured? Why? What do they think the manufacturer was seeking when choosing component producers (price, durability, style, etc.)?

Ask the groups to share their responses with the class, and keep a list on the board of the components and the suspected decision criteria. When the list is complete, ask your class to consider each component from the supplier's perspective. How can suppliers most effectively position themselves? How can they prevent themselves from becoming a simple price-based commodity?

Questions for Reflection:
- What are the advantages and disadvantages of buying components from outside manufacturers?
- How might the quality of components impact consumer perceptions of the whole product? Do brand name components change your purchasing decisions (e.g. "Intel inside," or "Made with Hershey's chocolate")?
- What are the ethical implications of "Made in America" labels for products manufactured with a large percentage of foreign components?

Outsourcing

Purpose:
> To highlight the impact of outsourcing on the key parties involved

Background:
> Despite a number of hiccups, "off-shoring" (or outsourcing overseas) remains a powerful, well-publicized trend in our economy. However, many companies also engage in more traditional outsourcing, sometimes laying-off individual employees or departments and then rehiring some of those people as independent contractors to perform the same services. This quick, discussion-based exercise is designed to help students examine the impact of this phenomenon.

Relationship to Text:
> Outsourcing (page 200)

Estimated Class Time:
> About 5-10 minutes

Preparation/Materials:
> None needed

Exercise:
> Share with your class that companies sometimes choose to lay-off individuals and then rehire those people as independent contractors to perform the same services (examples range from janitors to copy editors). Ask your students to identify the advantages and disadvantages of this kind of outsourcing, both for the firm and for the individuals involved. Help them understand that an entrepreneurial spirit and a strong marketing plan can transform these circumstances into a significant opportunity for the laid-off workers.

Questions for Reflection:
- Should marketing ever be outsourced? When? Why?

The Business Buying Process

Purpose:
> To trigger student thinking about personal sales in the B2B market

Background:
> Given that multiple parties are usually involved in significant B2B purchases, suppliers often use a team-based sales approach. The purpose is typically twofold: 1) to demonstrate the importance of the account to key decision-makers and 2) to cover more fully the range of decision influencers. This exercise is designed to help students better understand team-based B2B selling through role-playing.

Relationship to Text:
> Team Selling (page 209)

Estimated Class Time:
> About 20 – 30 minutes

Preparation/Materials:
> You might want to make a copy of the scenario and goals (below) for each student.

Exercise:
> Divide your class into no more than five groups (please note that this exercise works best for classes that have fewer than 40 students). Distribute the sales scenario:
>
> Scenario: You are a relatively new sales representative for a large cable programmer, and your key goal for the year is to convince the large cable systems in your area to carry your company's new cable network. You have just secured a five-minute appointment with Chris, the director of programming for your largest system. You haven't ever met Chris in person, and you know that no one from your company has called on this system for quite some time (the last person to handle your territory was fired for poor customer service). Your manager—thrilled that you generated this opportunity—has decided to accompany you to this brief meeting.
>
> Goal: In the next five minutes your group—representing the sales team—must prepare the sales representative and the sales manager to fully leverage the chance to sell your network to this pivotal system.
>
> Instruct each group to choose a sales rep and a manager to role-play the sales call for the class. For the sake of fairness, you may want to role-play the client (Chris) for every group.
>
> After each role-play, ask the class to identify the strengths of the approach and the opportunities for improvement. Encourage them to consider the following issues: Was the goal of the sales call clear? Did they attempt to accomplish too much or too little? Did they build rapport? Did they identify the client's needs? Did they identify others parties

who would influence the programming decision? Did they establish clear next steps? Did they respect the client's time? Most classes develop a surprising range of approaches to this fun exercise.

Questions for Reflection:
- In what situations would team selling be most effective? Could it ever be counter-productive?
- What are the benefits and drawbacks of a career in B2B sales?

Chapter 7
Serving Global Markets

Purpose:
To highlight a key challenge in global e-commerce

Background:
According the US Census Bureau "Population Clock," (a fun page of the mail site at http://www.census.gov/main/www/popclock.html), the US population is only 4.6% of the world population. This small (and declining) percentage reinforces the importance of global marketing to the long-term success of US companies, and the Web is an obvious way for even small companies to reach international markets. However, there are some major hurdles to crossing the US border, and this exercise is designed to highlight one of those challenges.

Relationship to Text:
The Importance of Global Marketing (page 221)

Estimated Class Time:
Less than 10 minutes

Preparation/Materials:
Each student will need paper and pen/pencil.

Exercise:
Ask your students to identify the key challenges for worldwide e-commerce. Most classes focus on issues with language, shipping and promotion, with less consideration for a growing and costly problem: credit card fraud. Share with them a recent study, which indicates that more than 40% of all credit card fraud against US companies online is committed by overseas offenders. Overall, international credit card fraud rates are about four times higher than domestic rates.

A quick quiz is a fun way to highlight this issue. Ask each student to number a paper from one to five, and to write their guesses for the countries that initiate the greatest number of fraudulent purchases. Then ask them to number from one to five again, and to write their guesses for the countries that initiate the *lowest* number of fraudulent purchases. Answers:

Highest rate of fraudulent credit card orders:
1) The former Yugoslavia
2) Nigeria
3) Romania
4) Pakistan
5) Indonesia

Lowest rate of fraudulent credit card orders:
1) New Zealand
2) Switzerland
3) Japan
4) France
5) Italy

Share the answers and tally scores by a show of hands. Why do your students think credit card fraud is so much higher in orders initiating from overseas? How can companies protect themselves?

Questions for Reflection:
- Given the cost of protecting against credit card fraud, does the Web really offer a level playing field for small and large companies?
- Should smaller e-commerce companies simply not accept orders from overseas? Why or why not?

Source: Sullivan, Bob, "Foreign Fraud Hits E-Commerce Firms Hard," MSNBC, April 1st, 2004, http://www.msnbc.msn.com/id/4648378/

The International Social/Cultural Environment

Purpose: To demonstrate the importance of knowing the international social/cultural environment

Background: Students often enjoy examples of marketing gone wrong, and the international examples can be both revealing and amusing. This exercise is designed to illustrate how sloppy preparation regarding the international social/cultural environment can undermine marketing effectiveness.

Relationship to Text: International Social/Cultural Environment (page 228)
Estimated Class Time: About 10 minutes
Preparation/Materials: None needed

Exercise: Share with your class these interesting examples of marketing communication issues. Some are actual gaffs and some are simply potential problems.
- In the mid-1990s, Panasonic licensed "Woody Woodpecker" as the Internet guide for the browser on a Japanese PC. But they stopped the launch the day before it happened, because someone pointed out their advertising slogan might cause some embarrassment: "Touch Woody, the Internet Pecker"
- Ikea promotes a mobile workbench called the "Fartfull," which suggests mobility in Swedish, but has very different implications in English (a very common second language throughout Europe and much of the world).
- The Volkswagen Jetta has done reasonably well in Italy, considering that "Jetta" is pronounced "Letta," which means misfortune, bad luck, or throw-away, depending on the dialect.
- Foreign companies over the years have introduced product after product into Germany (e.g. Irish Mist liquor, Silver Mist Rolls Royce). All have had issues, since "mist" translates roughly into "dung," or "manure."
- *Reed Business News* re-launched itself a couple of years ago with the slogan "If it's news to you, it's news to us." Not surprisingly they replaced the slogan after a few days.
- A sign in a Japanese hotel read, "You are invited to take advantage of the chambermaid."
- A sign in a Rome laundry read, "Ladies, leave your clothes here, and spend the afternoon having a good time."

Ask your class how these kinds of mistakes can happen. Help them understand that the most significant issues with translation are not always apparent in a dictionary…they often stem from slang words, dialects, or colloquialisms, which are a bit more difficult to research.

Questions for Reflection:
- Can cultural differences also cause marketing gaffs? What are some examples? (Possibilities include perceptions of time, gift giving, gender roles, gestures, etc.)
- How can companies prepare their marketers to avoid cultural mistakes? Is hiring locally usually a good solution? Why or why not?

Source: Texan, Tex, "Marketing Translation Mistakes," *Internationalization, Localization, Standards, and Amusements*, I18nGuy.com, http://www.i18nguy.com/translations.html

Bribery

Purpose:
To help students understand the implications of the *Foreign Corrupt Practices Act*

Background:
While US companies are explicitly forbidden from paying bribes by the *Foreign Corrupt Practices Act*, bribery remains an accepted business practice in many parts of the world. Ironically, many of the countries with the highest growth potential have the highest level of corruption. This exercise is designed to more fully explore the ethics and implications of the US position (and students typically have very strong feelings about these issues).

Relationship to Text:
International Political/Legal Environment (page 230)

Estimated Class Time:
About 15 minutes

Preparation/Materials:
None needed

Exercise:
Divide your class into groups of 3-5 students. Give the groups 5-10 minutes to develop a position on whether or not we should change the laws that prohibit bribery. Reconvene as a class, and ask your students to indicate via a show of hands, how they feel individually about this issue, *regardless of their group's position*. Using the material they developed in their groups, write a list on the board of the pros and cons for each position. Possibilities include: precedent, competitiveness, national morality, etc.

Follow-up questions: Do they think the law will ever change? Why or why not? Are "almost-bribes" (tickets to the Lakers, a donation to your favorite charity, large holiday fruit basket) OK? Where should the line be drawn?

Questions for Reflection:
- Given that bribes are not an option, how can American companies effectively compete in countries where bribes are an accepted practice? (This is a great place to emphasize the importance of innovation and customer service.)
- Could the *Foreign Corrupt Practices Act* suggest to other countries an attitude of "Our way is better than your way, so you need to adapt to us"? Why or why not? (Heads up: This question often leads to an intense political discussion, which may not be a fit for every class.)

Global Marketing Strategy

Purpose:
To help students apply marketing strategy concepts to "real-world" situations

Background:
Global marketing strategies can seem a bit abstract to many students. This exercise is designed to make the strategies seem more concrete, by giving students a chance to apply them to companies that they know.

Relationship to Text:
Going Global (page 238)

Estimated Class Time:
About 20-25 minutes

Preparation/Materials:
Each group will need unlined paper and pencil/pen

Exercise*:
Divide your students into groups of 5-7 people. Direct each team to select a company—familiar to everyone in the group—that could benefit from promoting its products to the Chinese market in conjunction with the 2008 Olympics in Beijing. Which strategy would make the most sense: straight extension, product or promotion adaptation, dual adaptation, or product invention? Why? Ask each group to create a print ad that reflects their ideas (English language copy is fine).

Reconvene as a class and ask the groups to share their strategic recommendations and their print ads. Which does the class think would work best? Why?

Questions for Reflection:
- What product categories are most likely to succeed in the Chinese market? Why?
- What are other issues to consider with regard to the Chinese market? (Possibilities span the spectrum of the global marketing environment, with particular emphasis on social/cultural, economic, and political/legal.)

---

*This exercise was adapted from the text.

More Global Marketing Strategy

Purpose:

To explore the strategic challenge of piracy in international markets

Background:

Piracy of intellectual property is a potentially crippling issue for key American exports, including software, movies, and music. While the problem is abating somewhat, it remains particularly acute in the huge, growing Asian markets. This exercise is designed to help students explore their strategic options in response to piracy of intellectual property.

Relationship to Text:

Developing an International Marketing Strategy (page 243)

Estimated Class Time:

About 15 minutes

Preparation/Materials:

You may want to make each student a copy of the scenario and goals below.

Exercise:

Share with your class this startling information from a recent *Newsweek Global Enterprise** issue: The percentage of software in use that is pirated (as of 2002) is 39% worldwide, and 92% (!!!) in China. With that in mind, divide your class into groups of 3-5, and ask them to consider the following scenario:

Scenario

You and your peers are the marketing team for a medium-sized software company, with a unique product that helps businesses save significant dollars in their payroll function. While your company has experienced success both at home and abroad, your division in China has yet to turn a profit after three years of operation. The problem is almost certainly piracy. Senior management, committed to keeping this division open, has charged your team with developing a strategy.

Goals

In the next 10 minutes you and your team must develop a list of strategic options for how your China division can handle the piracy issue in a way that will build the business long term.

Reconvene as a class, and ask each group to share their favorite three options. You may want to list them on the board, so that the class can develop a consensus on how to best approach this hot issue. (According to the *Global Enterprise** article, Microsoft has recently decided to approach the issue with a new strategy that focuses on partnerships with the government and large corporations, rather than on punitive measures against pirates.)

Questions for Reflection:
- Does it ever make sense from an ethical standpoint to use pirated software? When? Why?
- Do any of your peers download music? How have downloading habits changed over the past couple of years? Why? Has greater awareness of ethical issues played a role?

Source: Schafer, Sarah, "Microsoft's Cultural Revolution," *Global Enterprise, (Newsweek)*, June 28th, 2004, pages E10 - E16

Globalization and Cultural Exchanges

Purpose:
> To highlight the cultural shifts that have resulted from economic globalization

Background:
> During the past 25 years, the United States has been accused with increasing frequency of cultural imperialism, visible in the ubiquitous presence of fast food, hip-hop music, and Hollywood blockbusters. But the cultures of other countries have profoundly influenced the United States as well. This discussion-based exercise is designed to explore the cultural exchanges that inevitably result from economic globalization.

Relationship to Text:
> The US as a Target for International Marketers (page 246)

Estimated Class Time:
> About 10 minutes

Preparation/Materials:
> None needed

Exercise:
> Discussion Questions:
> - Ask your class for examples of how American culture has spread to other countries around the world. American students who have traveled are a great source of information, along with international students, if you have any.
> - Ask them how U.S. products have been modified, if at all, to suit other cultures. One interesting example is the film *Pearl Harbor*, marketed in the U.S. as a war movie and in Japan (where it was also a hit) as a love story. If you have computer projection, you may also want to take your students through the McDonald's Website (http://www.mcdonalds.com), which shows how key foods have been modified in other countries (e.g. seaweed fries and red-bean sundaes in Hong Kong).
> - Now ask for examples of how other countries have influenced U.S. culture. You may need to kick off the discussion with a few examples of your own, but once they get started, most classes easily develop long (and interesting!) lists. Possibilities include: Salsa dancing, Pokeman, soccer, ultra-lightweight cell phones, import beers, U-2, sushi, etc.

Questions for Reflection:
> - Does American culture help or hinder acceptance of foreign products? How?
> - Given the cultural exchanges spurred by globalization, are we in danger of developing a homogenous, vanilla world culture? Why or why not?

Chapter 8
Marketing Research, Decision-Support Systems, and Sales Forecasting

Marketing Research

Purpose:
To introduce marketing research through hands-on experience

Background:
Marketing research is the foundation of successful marketing, yet many students find the topic somewhat dry. This exercise is designed to introduce marketing research in a way that sparks student interest while previewing the basic concepts from the chapter.

Relationship to Text:
Chapter Overview (page 258)

Estimated Class Time:
About 25 minutes

Preparation/Materials:

You'll need to buy one package each of 4-5 different brands of chocolate chip cookies. Look for a variety of sizes and types, but beyond that, whatever is on sale will work. Put each type of cookie in a generic bag, and mark the bags Cookie A, B, etc. You'll also need either napkins or paper plates, and (if you're feeling especially nice!) a gallon or two of milk and paper cups.

Exercise*:

Announce that your class will be doing research on chocolate chip cookies. Working in small groups, their job is to develop and implement a research methodology to determine which cookie brand is the chippiest, which is the tastiest, and which is the overall best. They will need to report to the class their results, their methodology, and their level of certainty. Divide them into groups, and give them about 15 minutes to work.

When the groups report to the class, write the results in a matrix on the board. Don't tell them how the letters correspond to actual brands until the whole class is finished. (Interestingly, store brands seem to do surprisingly well!)

Group discussion questions: Which factors were hardest to determine? Which were the easiest? Which answers were subjective, and which were objective? Why weren't everyone's answers the same? How could a marketer for one of the manufacturers use this information? Encourage them to consider issues such as target market (are college students really an important target market for chocolate chip cookies?) and sample size (are the results from just one class projectable to the larger population?). When you do share the actual brands, ask them if there were any surprises. Why?

Questions for Reflection:
- Given that all marketing research techniques have limitations, why is it important to invest in research? How do you know when you have enough information?
- What role (if any) should intuition or "gut feel" play in marketing research? Why?

* Source: Sharon H. Ulanoff, Ph.D., Associate Professor, Elementary Reading and Bilingual Education, California State University, Los Angeles

The Marketing Research Process

Purpose: To help students apply the marketing research process

Background: On-going marketing research can play a significant role in keeping a business viable over the long term. This exercise is designed to help students understand how to approach the research process by applying it to a specific situation.

Relationship to Text: The Marketing Research Process (page 260)

Estimated Class Time: About 20 minutes

Preparation/Materials: You may want to copy the scenario and challenge (below) for each student.

Exercise:
After you have reviewed the material on the marketing research process, divide your class into groups of 3-5 students, and distribute the scenario outlined below:

Scenario
You and your partners are the owners of an upscale nightclub called *Amnesia Nights* on Sunset Boulevard in Hollywood, California. When you opened the club two years ago, it quickly became a trendy hotspot, attracting crowds of partiers in their 20s and 30s, plus a fair share of celebrities on the weekend evenings. However, in the last six months, attendance has declined significantly. You know that some clubs have a short (yet glamorous!) lifespan, but you are determined to be part of the scene for years to come. You have decided that the first step in recovering from the slump is marketing research.

The Challenge
You and your team have ten minutes to develop your ideas for marketing research by responding to the following questions:
- What primary and secondary information would you seek? Why?
- Who would be your research subjects? Why? How would you find them?
- What research methods would you use (e.g. surveys, focus groups, etc.)? Why?
- What are the advantages and disadvantages of your approach?

The teams will need to work quickly, but the time limit works well because they often generate their best ideas for this project in the first few moments. Ask each group to share their responses with the class, and encourage them to evaluate the merits of each approach honestly, but respectfully. By the end of the discussion, they should have a strong understanding of both the potential value and the limitations of marketing research.

Questions for Reflection
- Which steps of the marketing research process differ based on the target audience?
- Does product category affect the marketing research process? If so, how?

Sampling Techniques

Purpose:
> To highlight the difference between probability and non-probability samples

Background:
> Some students have difficulty distinguishing between probability and non-probability samples in actual practice. This quick, discussion-based exercise is designed to highlight the difference.

Relationship to Text:
> Sampling Techniques (page 266)

Estimated Class Time:
> Less than 10 minutes

Preparation/Materials:
> None needed

Exercise:
> Ask your class if they are a representative sampling of the school. At first many students will nod, but after a moment or two they usually begin to realize that they are not. Ask them to identify how they might be different from the general student body (business majors, time of day, employment status, etc.). Then, ask how you could collect a true random sample of students (they typically develop a variety of sound approaches). Finally, ask if it would ever make sense to use one class of students for marketing research. They should be able to identify several viable scenarios.

Questions for Reflection:
- What are the advantages and disadvantages of convenience samples?
- When are convenience samples likely to be "enough"?
- What are some specific situations that would call for a census rather than a sample? Rationale?

Primary Research Methods

Purpose:
To demonstrate a useful projective research technique

Background:
While gathering information through traditional marketing research methods (surveys, focus groups, etc.) can produce excellent results, using projective techniques can yield insights that respondents may find tough to articulate directly. This exercise is designed to give your students experience with a specific projective research method.

Relationship to Text:
Primary Research Methods (page 267)

Estimated Class Time:
About 10 minutes

Preparation/Materials:
You'll need to have either dry erase markers or pieces of chalk for five people.

Exercise:
Ask your students to brainstorm a list of 5-10 different cars that they know and like. Then, request five volunteers and invite them to the board. Ask each one to choose a car from the list, and then to draw a picture of how that car would look if it were a person (assure them that stick figures are fine). Ask them also to complete either a speech or a thought bubble. (For example, a classic VW beetle might be a young male "granola" type person, with a speech bubble that says "Groovy!")

When the drawings are complete, ask the volunteers to briefly describe their person's appearance, character traits, profession, and lifestyle. (For example, is the person uptight, friendly, geeky, handsome, or smooth? Does he or she live at home, share an apartment with friends, or own a mansion in the hills?)

After the presentations, ask the class to analyze the results. How would this information be helpful to market researchers? What did they learn that might not be as clear by asking more straightforward questions? In what product categories would projective research be most helpful? (It tends to work best for visible products that people identify with themselves in a personal way. Examples include spas, vacation destinations, computers, and alcoholic beverages.)

Questions for Reflection:
- How valid are projective techniques?
- How could you use these methods in conjunction with other types of research?

Garbology

Purpose:
> To explore a rather unorthodox method of primary research

Background:
> The text indicates that modern marketing research emerged more than a hundred years ago, due in large part to a study of garbage for Campbell Soup. The field of garbology—defined by the American Marketing Association as *the study of consumer behavior and preferences for food and products by examining...items found in the trash and garbage*—continues to play a small but significant role in marketing research today. This quick discussion exercise is designed to introduce students to garbology and its various uses.

Relationship to Text:
> Primary Research Methods (page 167)

Estimated Class Time:
> Less than 10 minutes

Preparation/Materials:
> You may want to do a quick Google search to determine whether searching garbage without permission in your state is legal.

Exercise:
> Share the definition of garbology with your students. (Be prepared for a lot of groans...in fact, if you want to tease them a bit, you could suggest that this exercise involves doing a survey of the garbage can in your classroom!)
>
> Ask them to brainstorm some ways that information collected through garbology could be useful to marketers (e.g. recycling habits, beer consumption, fast-food leftovers). Help them see the benefits of tracking what people *do* (rather than what they *say* they do) by studying their trash. Then, encourage them to consider the ethical implications of this approach. Does it need to involve some level of deceit? Why or why not? Does it violate privacy? How could these issues be resolved?

Questions for Reflection:
- Would garbology be more effective in conjunction with other types of research? Why or why not? What are some examples?

Chapter 9
Market Segmentation, Targeting, and Positioning

Market Segmentation

Purpose:
    To introduce the key chapter topics in a memorable way

Background:
    As the target audience for an overwhelming number of well-funded marketing campaigns, college students tend to know more than they think they know about market segmentation, targeting, and product positioning. This exercise is designed to transform that passive knowledge into active understanding.

Relationship to Text:
    Chapter Overview (page 288)

Estimated Class Time:
    Less than 10 minutes

Preparation/Materials:
    A marker and whiteboard

Exercise:
    Ask your class to write down their favorite brand of athletic shoe, and the one most important reason they buy that brand. As they share their brands and their reasons, ask a volunteer to keep a list on the board, categorized by brand. Before long, a profile of the market—divided into relatively clear segments—will begin to emerge, along with some positioning information for each brand. Going a step further, students often notice similarities among their peers who buy each brand, which demonstrates the target market for each shoe in a very vivid way. Help them recognize the key segmentation variables for their market profile (keeping in mind that the variables that emerge for each class tend to differ somewhat).

Questions for Reflection:
- Why is it important to segment a market?
- Is it better for a business to be a big fish in a small pond, or a small fish in a big pond? Why?

Differences Among Segments

Purpose: To highlight differences among market segments

Background: Long-term marketing success depends on knowing your market—understanding how and why the segments you target are different from all the others. Sometimes an astute marketer will uncover significant variation among segments that initially appear very similar, which can lead to significant opportunity. This exercise is designed to highlight the potential for unexpected differences in a memorable way.

Relationship to Text: The Role of Market Segmentation (page 289)

Estimated Class Time: About 10 minutes

Preparation/Materials: Each student will need paper and pen/pencil

Exercise*:   Ask your students to take out a paper and number from one to ten. Then, tell them that you will read them a list of Australian words. Their job is to write the American equivalent.

Australian Word	American Equivalent
1. Ankle biter	Small child
2. Boomer	Kangaroo
3. Cheese and Kisses	Wife
4. Earbasher	Bore
5. Pokies	Slot Machines
6. Sheila	Young Woman
7. Amber Fluid	Beer
8. Brolly	Umbrella
9. Grasshopper	Tourist
10. Tomato Sauce	Ketchup

Let them grade their own quizzes, and share the results with the class via a show of hands (a 20% success rate is surprisingly common). Then ask them how this quiz relates to marketing. Most classes quickly recognize the implications for targeting and positioning abroad, but help them also see that subtle language differences can be significant domestic opportunity as well. For instance, a recent *Newsweek* article suggests that targeting the Hispanic-American market is more effective when marketers use regional Spanish dialects and respond to the needs of specific market segments (source: Beith, Malcolm, "Targeting Hispanics," *Newsweek*, July 26, 2004).

Questions for Reflection:
- How can you uncover subtle but significant differences among market segments? What kind of marketing research is most helpful? Should the personal insights of the marketer also play a role? If so, how?

---

* This exercise was adapted from Baleja, Gregory, "What Language Do we Speak? Or Is English Really English?" *Great Ideas for Teaching Marketing*, http://www.swlearning.com/marketing/gitm/gitm4e07-01.html, accessed 7/20/04

Using Geographic Segmentation

Purpose:
To highlight an interesting angle regarding geographic segmentation

Background:
Many high profile geographic segmentation opportunities revolve around climate issues. However, *Forbes* magazine publishes an annual list of America's Best Cities for Singles, which suggests a different geographic segmentation opportunity. This exercise is designed to explore that prospect and the potential applications.

Relationship to Text:
Using Geographic Segmentation (page 291)

Estimated Class Time:
About 10-15 minutes

Preparation/Materials:
Each student will need paper and pen/pencil

Exercise:
Ask your students to take out a paper and write their guesses for the top ten positions on *Forbes* list of America's Best Cities for Singles. After you read the answers, direct them to score themselves based on the total number of correct cities that they included (not counting the order). Here are the cities:
1. Denver/Boulder
2. Washington/Baltimore
3. Austin
4. Atlanta
5. Boston
6. Los Angeles
7. Phoenix
8. New York
9. San Francisco

Then, ask them to brainstorm ideas for the ranking criteria. They may be interested (and surprised!) to learn the actual criteria:

1. Number of singles
2. Nightlife (number of bars, restaurants, nightclubs)
3. Culture (number of museums, pro-sports teams, live theaters, university students)
4. Cost of living alone
5. Job growth (5-year horizon)
6. Coolness (diversity and number of creative workers)

7. Buzz Factor (based on interactive polls with *Forbes* readers)

Regarding marketing implications, work as a class to develop a list of companies or product categories that could use this information (e.g. Apple i-Pods, e-Harmony online dating service, House of Blues, etc.). What are promotional techniques that would be cost effective across a set of concentrated geographic areas?

Questions for Reflection:
- How could these cities most effectively market themselves?
- What groups should they target? Certain types of businesses? Potential residents? Both?

Source: Dukcevich, Davide, Best Cities for Singles, Forbes.com, 6/25/04, http://www.forbes.com/2004/06/23/04singleland.html

Reaching Target Markets

Purpose:
To underscore the relationship between target marketing and promotion

Background:
When promotional strategies are executed effectively, the target market for a product should be readily apparent. The connection tends to be even stronger in highly competitive categories such as consumer products. This brief exercise is designed to help students recognize the link between target marketing and advertising.

Relationship to Text:
Strategies for Reaching Target Markets (page 307)

Estimated Class Time:
Less than 10 minutes

Preparation/Materials:
Choose five high-impact magazine ads from one or two competitive categories (possibilities include cars, cosmetics, cigarettes, athletic shoes, beer). If possible, mount the ads on a display board.

Exercise:
Show the ads to your class, and give them a couple of minutes to look and comment. Then, ask them to identify the target consumer group for each ad. How can they tell? Do the five ads represent all of the segments in the market? Which segments are missing? Which brands target those missing segments?

Questions for Reflection:
- When one company targets multiple segments with subtle differences, do they face danger of cannibalization and inefficiency?
- How can a company manage this issue effectively?

Source: This exercise was adapted from Cherry, Rosa, "Segmentation Assignment," *Great Ideas for Teaching Marketing*, http://www.swlearning.com/marketing/gitm/gitm4e04-05.html, accessed 7/20/04

Product Positioning

Purpose:
> To give students a chance to apply product positioning concepts

Background:
> Many students particularly enjoy articulating product positioning in new and exciting ways to capitalize on windows of opportunity in the marketplace. This exercise is designed to give them hands-on positioning experience.

Relationship to Text:
> Selecting and Executing a Strategy (page 308)

Estimated Class Time:
> About 15-20 minutes

Preparation/Materials:
> None needed

Exercise*:
> Divide your class into groups of 3-5 students, and ask each group to choose a product—familiar to all of them—that needs repositioning. (Possible categories: a beer brand, a pizza restaurant, cigarettes, your college, a television network, etc.) Then, direct them to just do it!
> - Step 1: Identify the current positioning (quick sentence)
> - Step 2: Sketch a positioning map that includes the key competitors
> - Step 3: Develop a new, unique positioning statement and slogan
>
> Ask each group to share their results with the class (and you can expect a remarkable level of creativity!).

Questions for Reflection:
- How do you know when a product needs to be repositioned?
- What are the risks of repositioning a product?
- What are examples of products that have succeeded and failed at repositioning?

*Adapted from the text

Chapter 10
Relationship Marketing, CRM, and One-to-One Marketing

Marketing Products We Love to Hate

Purpose: To explore the potential benefits of relationship marketing

Background: Since gaining initial customers is such a high-profile undertaking, many students give less thought to the more important function of building loyal, long-term relationships with current customers. This exercise is designed to highlight the importance of relationship marketing and to help students explore the range of relationship-building tools.

Relationship to Text: Chapter Overview (page 318)

Estimated Class Time: About 15 minutes

Preparation/Materials: None needed

Exercise:
Share with your class the 2004 Invention Index: Every year, the Lemelson-MIT program launches a study to gauge Americans' attitudes toward invention. In 2004, they studied inventions that Americans most hate but cannot live without. You may want to ask your students to guess the results before you share them. Cell phones were cited by 30% of the respondents, Alarm clocks by 25%, television by 23%, shaving razors by 14%. The remaining 8% included inventions such as microwaves, computers, and vacuum cleaners.

Next, divide your class into groups of 5-7 students, and ask each group to choose one brand among these essential yet despised inventions. Challenge them to develop at least five different ideas for how that company can build loyal, long-term relationships with their customers. Encourage them to be innovative, to think big. Brainstorming for a few moments is a great way to start.

After about ten minutes, ask the groups to share their ideas. You may be surprised at the level of creativity, which can set the tone for the whole chapter.

Questions for Reflection:
- Are there examples of companies in each of these categories that have managed to build strong, positive relationships with their customers? Why do so many fail to do so?
- From a profitability perspective, why does building relationships with current customers matter?

Source: 2004 Invention Index, Lemelson-MIT Program, January 21, 2004, http://web.mit.edu/invent/n-pressreleases/n-press-04index.html

Building Buyer-Seller Relationships

Purpose: To trigger student thinking about how to build customer relationships by adding value to goods and services

Background: In an increasingly competitive business environment, successful marketers build relationships with their customers through innovative ways of adding value to their products. The result can provide the basis for a significant competitive edge. This exercise is designed to help students begin thinking about *how* to build relationships by adding value, but without undermining profitability.

Relationship to Text: Building Buyer-Seller Relationships (page 325)
Estimated Class Time: About 15 minutes
Preparation/Materials: None needed

Exercise*:
Ask your students to share examples of businesses they know that offer added value (above and beyond their competitors). Encourage them to consider both small and large businesses, such as local buy-10-get-one-free programs and national airline frequent flyer programs.

Divide your class into groups of 5-7 students, and direct them to develop ideas for how each of the following businesses could add value without significantly eroding profits. Who should be the target customers for each of these benefits? Should they be offered to all customers? Why or why not?
- Real estate agency (Habitat for Humanity program donation in your name)
- Sandwich store (sandwich of the month contest)
- Trendy clothing Website (chat with experts on accessories, colors, etc.)
- Pediatrician's office (separate sick and well rooms, video games for kids)
- American Airlines (Selection of PPV movies at each seat)

Encourage them to be creative. Some natural history museums, for example, add value to the museum experience by offering youth groups the opportunity to camp overnight in the museum under the dinosaur bones (for a hefty fee, of course!).

After ten minutes, call time and ask each group to share their favorite concept. You'll likely get an entertaining mix of wacky and terrific ideas.

Questions for Reflection:
- About what percentage of a marketing promotion budget should be committed to these kinds of programs? Why?
- If you have a successful program, how could you proactively encourage word-of-mouth about it?

---

*This exercise was adapted from the text

Database Marketing

Purpose: To highlight opportunities to collect information for database marketing

Background:
Clearly, database information is crucial for relationship marketing; however, growing numbers of consumers in our fast-paced society are unwilling to spend time providing information for marketers. This exercise is designed to help students explore how they can use limited consumer patience to collect high quality information

Relationship to Text: Database Marketing (page 327)

Estimated Class Time: About 15 minutes

Preparation/Materials: None needed

Exercise:
Brainstorm as a class on opportunities for businesses to collect information from their customers. Examples might include questions at the cash register (e.g. "What is your zip code?"), questions on a mail-in warranty card, questions on Website registrations. Once you have a solid list, divide your students into groups of 3-5 people.

Direct the groups to assume that at each information-gathering opportunity, they can collect only five pieces of information; furthermore, that information must be gathered in a database-friendly format (close-ended questions). Ask them to consider each of the following businesses. What five questions would they ask for each?
- Electronics shop
- Nightclub
- Sports arena
- Hotel
- Hair salon

After about ten minutes request that a volunteer from each of five groups write their questions on the board. Then ask the class to contribute any additional questions that are significantly different from those already on the board. The overlap among the questions is usually huge.

Follow-up discussion: How would they use each piece of information? Would it be better to collect different information at each opportunity? Why or why not?

Questions for Reflection:
- What companies seem to be especially effective at database marketing? How do you know?
- What are information sources for database marketing beyond direct questions? What (if any) are the ethical implications of using this information?

Grassroots Marketing

Purpose: To help students stretch their creative capacity

Background:
Grassroots marketing—innovative and unconventional—tends to be highly effective…but only when it is based on a great idea. This exercise is designed to help students develop the creative skills that will be critical for their success.

Relationship to Text: Grassroots Marketing (page 329)

Estimated Class Time: About 15 minutes

Preparation/Materials:
Prepare a set of index cards, each with a random noun or short phrase. Possibilities include: mountaintop, calculator, video game, computer screen, mother, rabbit, running shoes, window screen, beach, etc. Make about twice as many cards as you have groups of 5-7 in your class.

Exercise:
Review with your students the text definition of grassroots marketing: "Strategies that are unconventional, nontraditional, not by the book, and extremely flexible." Warn them that this exercise will indeed be unconventional, but also lots of fun!

Divide your class into groups of 5-7 students, and announce that each group represents the management team of a local independent bookstore that faces increasing competition from the big national chains.

Ask each team to send a representative to choose a card from your stack. Then, challenge the groups to develop at least three grassroots marketing strategies that connect in some way to the word on their card (the wackier the connection the better!). For example, the word mountaintop may make them think of high altitude, which may make them think of creating a loft, which may make them think of offering weekly seminars in their loft for aspiring writers, etc.) Encourage them to relax, have fun, and be creative.

After about ten minutes, ask each group to present their favorite idea and how their idea connects to their word. To boost energy and excitement, you may want to have the class vote on the best strategy (but don't let any group vote for themselves). A little extra credit for the best concept adds remarkable motivation!

Questions for Reflection:
- What are some real-world examples of compelling grassroots marketing? (You may want to name a few of your own favorites to spark discussion.)
- If you owned your own business, how would you boost creativity among your marketing staff?

Retrieving Lost Customers

Purpose:
To highlight the importance of retrieving lost customers

Background:
Winning back lost customers is not a glamorous function, but it can be deeply satisfying. More importantly, retrieving lost or disgruntled customers can make a dramatic, positive difference in terms of profitability. This exercise is designed to help students explore ways to win back customers.

Relationship to Text:
Retrieving Lost Customers (page 331)

Estimated Class Time:
About 10 minutes

Preparation/Materials:
Recruit two vocal, articulate, and thick-skinned volunteers before you do this exercise. Give one the customer information and the other the cable system information, and spend a few moments helping them understand their roles. Make copies of both parts for the rest of the class.

Exercise:
Ask your two volunteers to wait outside, and announce to the rest of the class that this will be a role-playing exercise on retrieving lost customers at a cable system. Distribute the information below to the class, and read each part aloud.

Cable Customer: You have just called the cable system to disconnect your service. You have been unhappy with the cable system for months. The customer service reps are typically sullen and slow. Also, you deeply resent that anytime the cable people need to do anything with the cable box, you have to take half a day off work (and even then, they don't always show up in the four hour window they promised!). The last straw was that you wanted to add HBO in response to a flyer you received, but they told you that the 25% discount offer—which you only received last week—had expired. You haven't cancelled the service before now, because you don't want to deal with the hassle of setting up satellite TV, but today, you're mad enough to just do it. When you called to cancel, the customer service rep put you on-hold so you could speak with a specialist.

What would make you reconsider? First and foremost, you want to feel that the cable system understands your concerns. While you would love a big discount on your basic cable—plus free HBO for at least a few months—you would settle for simple receiving the 25% discount from your flyer. You will *only* reconsider if the customer retrieval specialist listens well to all your concerns, and offers you the 25% discount on HBO. Otherwise you will proceed with canceling.

Customer Retrieval Specialist

Your job is to win-back customers who have cancelled their cable service. Management will consider you successful by measuring both the number of customers you save, and average cost of saving each one. You have several options to offer customers if necessary: 1) free basic cable for up to six months, and 2) free HBO for up to a year. You are fairly new at your job, and you are deeply motivated to save as many customers as you can.

When your class understands both positions, spend a few moments brainstorming about how the customer retrieval specialist can succeed. Then, call in your volunteers, and begin the role-play!

Whether the customer retrieval specialist succeeds or fails, the discussion is usually rich. Ask your students what went well, and what could have gone better. Underscore the importance of listening to your customers *before* they defect.

Questions for Reflection:
- How can you increase listening and empathy skills among customer contact people, especially since they are often poorly paid?
- What are examples of companies that have done well at empowering their people to solve customer problems before customers defect? (High profile possibilities include the Ritz-Carleton and Nordstrom.)

Chapter 11
Product and Service Strategies

Goods-Services Continuum

Purpose:
To help students better understand the Goods-Services Continuum

Background:
The distinction between a good and a service can be somewhat confusing, since most products include some combination of the two. This exercise is designed to encourage students to engage in critical thinking regarding how products fit the goods-services continuum.

Relationship to Text:
What Are Goods and Services? —Goods-Services Continuum (page 352)

Estimated Class Time:
About 15 minutes

Preparation/Materials:
- Write a giant goods-services continuum line on the board. Number the line from one to ten, with "pure good" at the one and "pure service" at the ten:

    Pure good |-----|-----|-----|-----|-----|-----|-----|-----|-----| Pure service
             1   2   3   4   5   6   7   8   9 10

- Write the name of each company listed below on a small, folded piece of paper, so that students can choose at random.
- Consider preparing some small prizes (candy is always a hit).

Exercise:
Divide your class into groups of 5-7 people. For the sake of esprit de corps, give them a moment to choose names, and write them on the board. Then, direct the groups to decide where to place the following companies on the continuum (whole numbers only—no fractions allowed!), along with a strong rationale.
- Yahoo.com
- Dinner at an upscale restaurant
- eBay
- Starbucks coffee
- Neutrogena shampoo
- Chiropractor office
- Ski resort
- Shoes from Nordstrom
- H&R Block tax preparation
- Caribbean luxury cruise

Then the fun begins! Announce that each group starts with ten points (which you should track on the board). A volunteer from each team will choose a company at random (from your folded papers), write it on the continuum, and explain why the group assigned that placement.

Then, any other group can challenge the placement (one challenge per group). The challengers must provide their rationale, and the class votes on the outcome. If the challengers win, they take half the points of the group that presented, but if they lose, they must forfeit half their points to the other group. After each group has presented, the one with the most points wins. To encourage risk-taking, you may also want to offer a small prize to the group with the least number of points. Tootsie Rolls work great for both the winning and the losing groups.

Questions for Reflection:
- How would marketing strategies differ for products at either end of the continuum?
- Which end offers greater profit potential? Why?
- Do individual companies typically move along the spectrum? Why or why not?

Features of Services

Purpose:
> To highlight the concrete meaning of each feature of services

Background:
> Since few services are completely "pure," students are often quite puzzled about what the features of services actually mean, and how to apply them to real-world cases. This quick, discussion-based exercise is designed to clarify each of the features through concrete examples.

Relationship to Text:
> What Are Goods and Services? —Features of Services (page 353)

Estimated Class Time:
> Less than 5 minutes

Preparation/Materials:
> None needed

Exercise:
> Choose an example of a complex service—Disneyland and Disney World work especially well—and ask your class to determine whether it embodies each feature of a service. Be sure that they can justify their responses. The discussion quickly surfaces areas of confusion, which often leads to students explaining the features to each other (a nice dynamic). Many classes also "agree to disagree" on some features, which highlights the inherent blurriness of the product-service distinctions.

Questions for Reflection:
- Why does it matter whether your product is a good or a service? How (if at all) would the distinction affect marketing strategy?
- What is the biggest challenge in marketing services? Why?

The Full Range of Products

Purpose:
>To reinforce student understanding of different types of products

Background:
>This exercise is designed to focus student attention on product classification and the product life cycle in a way that they won't easily forget.

Relationship to Text:
>Classifying Goods and Services (page 355) and The Product Life Cycle (page 370)

Estimated Class Time:
>About 20 minutes

Preparation/Materials:
>You may want to make each student a copy of the list for the scavenger hunt (if not, you can simply write the list on the board, and ask them to copy it). Also, consider preparing some small prizes (e.g. candy).

Exercise:
>Announce to your class that they are about to embark on a product scavenger hunt, and they need to begin by dividing themselves into teams of 5-7 people. The first team to return with a complete set of products wins. Encourage them to be creative. The only rules are: 1) all products must be legal, 2) no product can meet more than one requirement, and 3) no team can spend any money. Here is the list:
>- A convenience product
>- A staple product
>- An emergency product
>- A shopping product
>- A specialty product
>- A business product
>- A truly excellent product
>- A completely terrible product
>
>Most teams take about 10 – 15 minutes. And while there usually is a clear winner, it is fun to give each team a chance to share their findings. Extra credit points and small candies both work well as prizes.

Questions for Reflection:
- What strategies did the teams use to collect the products? Which seemed to be most effective, and why?
- Do you believe that marketing works best in teams? Why or why not?

Quality as a Product Strategy

Purpose:
To explore the meaning of quality across a range of goods and services

Background:
Quality plays a critical role in the long-term success of any product; however, the *meaning* of quality varies significantly across product categories. This exercise is designed to help students understand the different dimensions of quality products.

Relationship to Text:
Quality as a Product Strategy (page 364)

Estimated Class Time:
About 10 minutes

Preparation/Materials:
None needed

Exercise:
Ask your class what product quality means. After they have shared some thoughts, ask them if the definition of quality changes depending on the type of business. You may want to illustrate this point with the example of a restaurant: A high quality meal at McDonald's is exactly the same as the meal you got last time, and the time before that, and the time when you were five years old. A high quality meal at a fine French restaurant is different every time you eat there. Quality service at McDonalds might mean a cheerful "Have a nice day!" while at a fine French restaurant, it might mean a silent, respectful nod.

Divide your class into groups of 4-5 people, and give each group five to ten minutes to define what quality means for each of the following categories:
- A visit to the dentist
- A computer
- A motorcycle
- A haircut
- A pair of blue jeans
- A cup of coffee
- A stereo system

Ask each group to share their results, and then ask the class as a whole to share what they think this means from a marketing perspective.

Questions for Reflection:
- What is the marketing impact of poor quality?
- Should you promote high quality, or should you let your high quality products speak for themselves? Why or why not?

Product Mix Decisions

Purpose:
> To highlight the thought process behind product mix decisions

Background:
> Developing and maintaining the right product mix is a challenging and exciting proposition for any company, especially given the significant implications for long-term profitability. This exercise is designed to give students a chance to explore product mix considerations for businesses that are familiar to them.

Relationship to Text:
> Product Mix Decisions (page 369)

Estimated Class Time:
> About 15 minutes

Preparation/Materials:
> None needed

Exercise:
> As a class, brainstorm a quick list of local businesses that your students know and like (a pizza place, a bookstore, a bar, etc.). Then divide the class into groups of 3-5 students, and direct each group to develop at least one line extension concept for each business.
>
> After about ten minutes (they'll need to work fast), ask each group to present their favorite idea to the class, along with the rationale. Vote as a class for the best idea (and don't let the groups vote for themselves!). If it makes sense in your town, you may want to suggest that the students meet with the business owner and present their idea, perhaps in exchange for some extra credit.

Questions for Reflection:
- What is the best source of ideas for line extensions? Why?
- What factors would any business need to consider before extending its product mix? Which considerations should be highest priority? Why?

Extending the Product Life Cycle

Purpose:
> To encourage your students to see old products in new ways

Background:
> As product life cycles in many categories condense into shorter timeframes, extending the product life cycle has become a critical issue. This exercise is designed to help your students explore the possibilities of new uses for familiar, established products (and it's also a lot of fun!).

Relationship to Text:
> Extending the Product Life Cycle (page 373)

Estimated Class Time:
> About 20 minutes

Preparation/Materials:
> You'll need to gather a set of ordinary household items, enough for each group of 3-5 to have something different. Possibilities include a fork, a clothespin, a coffee cup, a cloth napkin, a pencil, a manila folder, etc. (Having multiple groups with the same item will work, too, if you can only gather a few things.)

Exercise:
> Divide your class into groups of 3-5 students, and give each group one of the household items that you collected. Direct them to spend five minutes brainstorming as many alternative uses as possible for their item (e.g. a fork could be used as a hairbrush, or a manila folder could be used as a book cover). Encourage them to be as creative as they can—not to hold back any ideas (for some classes, you may need to review the rules of brainstorming).
>
> When you call time, give them a moment to identify their two or three favorite ideas. Ask each group to report those ideas to the class, and record their results on the board.
>
> Reconvene as a class for discussion. Which idea is the most practical? The most creative? The most silly? Could the silliest idea be made marketable? How?
>
> You may want to close by pointing out some new product successes that stem from marketing old products in new ways (e.g. baking soda as a refrigerator deodorizer, peanut butter as a squeezable snack in a tube, or Jell-O as Jigglers).

Questions for Reflection:
- When does it make sense to allow an old product to die, rather then trying to rejuvenate it? Why?
- Are any products immune from decline? Why or why not?

Chapter 12
Category and Brand Management, Product Identification, and New-Product Development

Examining Branding

Purpose: To highlight the characteristics of a powerful brand

Background:
Brand value, or brand equity, is essentially the value of a brand above and beyond the value of the tangible assets used to produce that brand. The text points out that studies have linked high brand equity to high profits and strong stock returns. This quick discussion exercise is designed to illustrate how a strong brand concept extends far beyond the product itself, speaking more directly to the needs and experiences of the target market.

Relationship to Text:
Managing Brands for Competitive Advantage (page 382)

Estimated Class Time:
Less than 10 minutes

Preparation/Materials:
None needed

Exercise:
Ask your students for examples of great brands. Why do they think that the brands they identified stand above the competition? Solicit from them the characteristics of great brands, and list those qualities on the board. Be sure they understand the importance of a clear, relevant positioning that speaks directly to consumers.

Then share with your students the following items:
- Charles Revson, founder of Revlon cosmetics, said, "In our factory, we make lipstick. In our advertising, we sell hope." What does this mean? How does this relate to the characteristics of great brands that the class just identified?
- A small group of ranchers in the West have earned certification as "predator friendly" producers, meaning that they have pledged not to kill predators who threaten their livestock. In trying to market this proposition to consumers, their program director commented, "No one's saying 'Buy my beef because we don't kill coyotes,' but 'Buy my beef because it's good for you and the environment.'" Why is the second proposition so much stronger than the first?

Questions for Reflection:
- What is the most effective starting point in creating a strong brand concept?
- Is a strong brand concept more important on the Internet? Why or why not?

Brand Names

Purpose:
> To underscore the varied origins of effective brand names

Background:
> A surprising number of students are planning to start their own businesses, so choosing the right name is understandably a hot topic for many of them. This exercise is designed to explore the genesis of successful brand names, in an effort to provide understanding and inspiration.

Relationship to Text:
> Brand Names and Brand Marks (page 388)

Estimated Class Time:
> About 20 minutes

Preparation/Materials:
> You will need to make a copy of the list of brands (below) for each student.

Exercise:
> Divide your students into groups of 3-5 students, and give each person the list of brands in the table below. Direct the teams to extrapolate different sources of brand names from the brands in the table (and encourage them to use any other brand names to support their thinking.)

Lunchables	Southwest Airlines
Great Western Bank	Nike
McDonald's	Apple
Dove shampoo	Dell
Weight Watchers	Kellogg
Marlboro	Tropicana
Vanguard	Ford Motor Company
Bank of America	Tide detergent
Cosmopolitan magazine	Hewlett Packard
Playboy	Gap
Subway	Reebok
Dreamworks	Amazon
US News and World Report	George Forman grills
Intel	Disney
Yahoo	Citibank
Victoria's Secret	Craftsman tools
American Airlines	Virgin Records
Watchovia	Google
E-Trade	Haagan Daz

Students seem to love this exercise, perhaps for its relevance to their own business plans. Categories that typically emerge include the following:

- Location-based—refers to either the area-served or the place of origin. Examples: Southwest Airlines, Bank of America
- Founder's name. Examples: Ford, Disney, McDonald's, Hewlett-Packard, Kellogg
- Descriptive or functional—describes what the product is or how it works. Examples: E-Bay, US News and World Report
- Evocative—communicates an engaging image. Examples: Yahoo, Craftsman, Virgin, Intel, Lunchables, Cosmopolitan

Questions for Reflection:
- Can a name fall into more than one category? What are some examples (e.g. E-Bay is both descriptive and evocative)?
- In the face of increasing competition, more and more names for recently established brands either describe the product's function or attempt to evoke an image (e.g. Yahoo, Amazon). Is there likely to be a backlash? Will founders' names be used at some point specifically to evoke a nostalgic image (e.g. Bob's Market)?

Trademarks

Purpose:
> To explore the value of trademarks

Background:
> Brand identifiers for many products go far beyond brand names, sometimes including symbols, packaging, colors, and other elements of trade dress. This exercise is designed to help students internalize the value of trademarks and trade dress, while flexing their creative muscles.

Relationship to Text:
> Trademarks (page 391)

Estimated Class Time:
> About 10 minutes

Preparation/Materials:
> Students will need paper and pen/pencil.

Exercise:
> Share the following brand identifiers with your class: McDonald's golden arches, the Merrill Lynch bull, the Nike Swoosh, the color brown for UPS, the bitten apple for Apple Computer. Help them brainstorm identifiers for additional brands.
>
> Then, break the class into groups of 5-7 students, and assign at least two identifiers to each group. Challenge them to develop alternatives for each brand, and encourage them to think as far outside the box as they can. Then, ask each group to sketch their favorite option, and to share it with the class as part of a print ad.
>
> While most classes develop very creative (sometimes wacky) alternatives, they will typically conclude that brand identifiers are a critical part of a brand's success and as such, are very deserving of legal protection.

Questions for Reflection:
- What role should the government play in protecting trademarks? Why?
- Should any trademark "knock-offs" be legal? Why or why not?

The Roles of Packaging

Purpose: To explore the various roles of packaging

Background:
In the face of increasing competition, packaging in today's market must accomplish a wide range of objectives. This exercise is designed to help students recognize and evaluate the multiple functions of packaging.

Relationship to Text: Packaging (page 393)

Estimated Class Time: About 15 minutes

Preparation/Materials:
Choose a kid's cereal with a hardworking package, and bring as many boxes as you have groups of 5-7 people. (This exercise also works if each group has a different brand of kids' cereal.) Students will also need unlined paper and pens or pencils.

Exercise:
Divide your class into groups of 5-7 people, and distribute the cereal boxes to each group. Give them about five minutes to determine all of the functions of the package. Possibilities include:
- Grabbing attention
- Conveying the product image
- Providing information about the product itself
- Communicating the nutrition facts
- Appealing to multiple audiences
- Promoting a free gift inside
- Entertaining kids during breakfast
- Demonstrating value
- Providing convenience

When you call time, ask the class to call out the functions, while you list them on the board.

Then, direct each group to determine which functions the package could do better, and to develop and sketch an improved version of the package to share with the class. To boost excitement, you may want to have them vote on the best new package, with a few extra credit points as an added incentive.

Questions for Reflection:
- Does packaging matter more for some categories than for others? Why?
- What are examples of products that use packaging to create a competitive edge?

New Product Idea Generation

Purpose:
>To help your students develop creative thinking processes for new product development

Background:
>Continual new product development is a critical success factor for most contemporary businesses. Idea generation is the first step in the process, and it requires a rare level of open-mindedness. This exercise is designed to provide a tool to stimulate fresh thinking in the idea generation stage.

Relationship to Text:
>Idea Generation (page 402)

Estimated Class Time:
>About 25 minutes

Preparation/Materials:
>You'll need to bring one or two large beach balls to class. You can find them in most toy stores for less than $2.00.

Exercise:
>Announce that your class will be (for the moment!) the new product development team for a small chain of coffee shops that faces increasing competition from Starbucks. Push aside the furniture, and ask them to form a large circle (if you have an especially large class, you may want to form 2-3 circles). Pull out the beach ball, and announce the game:
>
>>*Their job is to toss the beach ball around the circle. The beach ball must never stop moving and must never touch the ground. Each time the ball hits their hands, they must call out their first thought regarding coffee shops. Anyone who says nothing is out of the game.*
>
>Allow them to toss the ball for five or ten minutes, and write everything they say—from clever to ridiculous—on the board. When the flow of ideas abates, stop the ball, and read the list aloud to your class. Then, divide them into groups of 3-5 people, and direct each group to use the list to develop at least five new product ideas that will help their coffee shop compete. Ask them to share their favorite ideas with the class.

Questions for Reflection:
- Did the exercise with the beach ball stimulate creativity? Why or why not?
- What are other ways to spark out-of-the-box thinking?

Chapter 13
Marketing Channels and Supply Chain Management

Distribution Strategy

Purpose:
To demonstrate some key trade-offs in creating an effective distribution system

Background:
Unfortunately, most students seem to find distribution to be the least interesting of the marketing P's. While this exercise does not incorporate the complexity of most actual distribution decisions, it is designed to spark student interest in learning more about this crucial element of the marketing mix.

Relationship to Text:
Channel Strategy Decisions (page 421)

Estimated Class Time:
About 20 minutes

Preparation/Materials:
You'll need to bring to class a large bag of well-wrapped candies that don't get easily squished or broken. Tootsie Rolls, lollipops, or mini candy bars are all good choices. You'll also need a basket or box of some kind, about the size of a small household wastebasket. Place the basket at the front of the classroom—ideally on a desk or podium—and mark a spot in the back of the classroom.

Exercise:
Divide your class into groups of about 5 people, and direct each group to choose a "factory owner." Present each team with 25 candies and the scenario outlined below. Their job is to plan a distribution strategy that will maximize profits.

The Scenario: You are the owner of a candy factory and you just produced 25 candies. Your goal is to work with your team to earn as much money as possible by distributing your candy to your consumers, who will pay $1.00 for each candy that they receive. Your consumers are represented by the basket at the front of the room; only the candies deposited in the basket will count as successful deliveries. You will not receive any money for candies that do not land in the basket, and you will not have a chance to retrieve them and try again (no second chances in the real world of distribution!).

The Rules: When you begin distributing your candy, you cannot move from where your teacher places you, and you cannot move the consumer basket. You may place as many of your teammates as you like between you and the consumer to help distribute your candy, but you must pay each one $.20 per piece of candy that they help distribute. Your helpers cannot move from where you place them.

Give each team about 5 minutes to plan their strategy, and direct them to distribute their candies one at a time originating from the spot you designated at the back of the room. When each team finishes, tally their profits.

Some teams will probably opt to have their owner toss the candies from the factory to the consumer. Those candies that make it into the basket will be highly profitable, but many will miss the basket (unless the factory owner has particularly good aim). Other teams will opt to have varying numbers of distributors. Clearly, large numbers will increase their accuracy, but decrease their profits; small numbers will decrease their accuracy, but increase their profits. The team with the highest profits wins the game.

After you complete the game and divide the candies, ask your class to consider how this exercise relates to the distribution function of marketing. The link between the number of distributors and the accuracy of distribution will likely be clear, but encourage them to also consider the exceptions. Costco, for instance, sells many of their products directly from the producer to the consumer—a very short distribution chain—and they hit their target with enormous accuracy.

Questions for Reflection:
- How does the product itself affect distribution decisions (e.g. upscale furniture versus cheap candy)?
- How do the characteristics of the target market affect distribution decisions?

Distribution Intensity

Purpose:
To highlight the options and trade-offs regarding distribution intensity

Background:
Distribution intensity within product categories varies more widely than many students expect. This exercise is designed to illustrate the range by asking students to generate specific examples of each intensity level within a number of categories.

Relationship to Text:
Determining Distribution Intensity (page 422)

Estimated Class Time:
About 15 minutes

Preparation/Materials:
You might want to write each of the categories listed below on the board.

Exercise:
After you cover the section on distribution intensity, divide your students into pairs, and instruct them to brainstorm examples of companies with intensive, selective, and exclusive distribution for each of the following categories:
- Baked goods (cakes, cookies, donuts)
- Cars
- Clubs
- Men's dress suits
- Cosmetics
- Blue jeans
- Computers
- Writing pens
- Restaurants

After no more than ten minutes, ask them to call out examples for each category, and write them on the board (you'll find that some were much harder for them than others!). If they don't immediately see it, help your students understand the close links between distribution intensity, product image, and price.

Questions for Reflection:
- What factors should a company consider when determining distribution intensity? Why?
- When can distribution intensity spark horizontal channel conflict? Why? (Consider franchises and sales territories.)

Channel Conflict

Purpose:
To vividly demonstrate the potential sources of vertical channel conflict

Background:
Teamwork and trust are essential for marketing channels to attain maximum efficiency. But since channel members are often independent organizations, some level of conflict is inevitable. This exercise is designed to illustrate the potential causes and consequences of vertical channel conflict.

Relationship to Text:
Vertical Conflict (page 426)

Estimated Class Time:
About 20 minutes

Preparation/Materials:
None needed

Exercise*:
Divide your class into three sections, and ask the students in each section to divide themselves into smaller groups (4-5 people). Then assign each section the role of retailer, wholesaler, or producer. Instruct the groups to brainstorm two lists of potential gripes directed toward each of the other two sections. For instance, the groups in the section with the producer role should develop one list of potential complaints for wholesalers, one for retailers.

After about five minutes, reconvene as a class, and ask a volunteer from one of the sections to direct a complaint to one of the other sections. Ask the other section to respond, and then to launch their own complaint. With very little prodding, students step into their respective roles. The responses and counter-responses begin to fly, as they pass blame from one channel member to another. With this playful animosity, students quickly understand how easily channel conflict escalates, and how quickly relationships can break down.

Questions for Reflection:
- What are some strategies to avoid unhealthy channel conflict?
- Can some level of channel conflict be productive? Even creative? What are some hypothetical examples?

---

*This exercise was adapted from Fujimoto, Wanda, "Who's to Blame? A Channel Conflict Exercise," Great Ideas for Teaching Marketing, http://www.swlearning.com/marketing/gitm/gitm4e02-10.html, accessed 8/7/04

Transportation Modes

Purpose:
To explore the strengths and drawbacks of various transportation modes

Background:
Clearly, choosing the best transportation mode—or combination of modes—involves trade-offs that are not always obvious. This exercise is designed to highlight these tradeoffs by examining transportation options for a range of products.

Relationship to Text:
Major Transportation Modes (page 435)

Estimated Class Time:
About 10 minutes

Preparation/Materials:
None needed

Exercise:
Divide your class into groups of 3-5 students. Direct the groups to determine the best mode of transportation (or combinations of modes) to transport the following products from Amsterdam to Topeka, Kansas.
- Fresh fish
- Tee shirts for a boutique
- Office supplies
- Sugar
- Luxury cars
- Fresh flowers
- Uncut diamonds
- Legal documents
- Digital cameras
- Fresh peaches

After about five minutes, instruct the groups to call out their answers, and be sure that they explain their thinking. What are the pros and cons of each choice? (Typically the richest discussion emerges from the points of disagreement.) What are some general guidelines that they can develop? (Possibilities: airfreight makes sense for trendy products, shipping makes sense for heavy products, etc.)

Questions for Reflection:
- Do the same transportation modes always make sense for a given category? Why or why not? What factors would lead to differences?
- What information do you need to determine the right transportation modes?

Distribution Packaging

Purpose: To give your students hands-on experience with packaging for shipment

Background: Creating the best package for transporting products is distinctly unglamorous, but the right package can make a significant difference to the bottom line. This exercise is designed to demonstrate several of the key issues in developing effective, efficient packaging for shipment (and to have some fun!).

Relationship to Text: Protective Packaging and Materials Handling (page 440)

Estimated Class Time: About 30 minutes

Preparation/Materials: For each group of 5-7 people, you'll need a roll of masking tape, about 20 plastic drinking straws, a stack of 8-1/2 X 11 inch paper, and two raw eggs. You'll also need some newspaper (or plastic tarp) to cover part of the floor, a chair, and a tape measure.

Exercise*:

Ask if any of your students have purchased or received a product that has been damaged in shipment. Help them understand that this is not only frustrating, but also creates disgruntled customers, bad word-of-mouth, and additional costs to the distributor.

Announce that their challenge is to use their ingenuity to create the perfect package for shipping a very fragile product: raw eggs. Each group must use nothing but paper, drinking straws, and masking tape. The minimum specification for the package is that it must be able to be dropped from a height of eight feet without breaking the egg. The winning package will meet this specification at the lowest cost per package.

Allow the groups to use as much of the materials as they need, but let them know that on their final product you will calculate the cost of all of their materials:
- Tape: $20/inch
- Straws: $100/straw
- Paper: $5/sheet

Since each group has two eggs, they may test their package with one, and use the other for their actual product demonstration.

Give the groups 15 minutes to complete their carriers, and then reconvene as a class for the demonstrations. (To keep things fair, you should drop each of the packages—over the newspaper, of course—from the specified height.) Collect the packages with unbroken eggs, and in front of the class estimate the cost of materials for each carrier. The carrier with an unbroken egg and the lowest cost of goods is the winner.

Questions for Reflection:
- In developing packaging, must there be a trade-off between efficiency and effectiveness? If so, what factors should you consider in determining the final equation?
- Should marketers tolerate *any* breakage in shipment? Why or why not?

Source: Adapted from Herrenkohl, Roy C. (2004). Becoming a Team, Mason, Ohio: South-Western, page 114.

Chapter 14
Direct Marketing and Marketing Resellers: Retailers and Wholesalers

Wal-Mart: Retailing Giant

Purpose:
To examine the strategy behind Wal-Mart's retailing success

Background:
Wal-Mart has generated a number of controversies, but the bottom-line success of their retailing approach is undisputed. This exercise is designed to help students understand and evaluate the strategic business philosophy that Wal-Mart espouses.

Relationship to Text:
Chapter Overview (page 448)

Estimated Class Time:
About 15-20 minutes

Preparation/Materials:
You may want to copy the summary of "Sam's Rules For Building A Business," listed below.

Exercise:

If you think they wouldn't know, ask your students to guess the largest company in the world based on total revenue, as measured by *Fortune* magazine. Consider sharing a few details:

With over $260 billion in revenue, Wal-Mart, a retailer, has been the largest company in the world since 2001. The other companies in the top five in 2004 are British Petroleum, Exxon Mobil, Royal Dutch/Shell Group, and General Motors. In fact, the second retailer on the list, France's Carrefour, doesn't appear until number 22, and other major retailers—a tiny fraction of the top 100—lag even further behind.

Given this success, the founder of Wal-Mart, Sam Walton, was often asked his secret. In his 1992 book, he shared "Sam's Rules for Building a Business," which the company claims as a guiding philosophy even today. Summary:

1) Commit to your business. Believe in it more than anybody else.
2) Share your profits with all your Associates, and treat them as partners.
3) Motivate your partners. Money and ownership alone aren't enough.
4) Communicate everything you possibly can to your partners.
5) Appreciate everything your Associates do for the business.
6) Celebrate your successes. Find some humor in your failures.
7) Listen to everyone in your company. And figure out ways to get them talking.

8) Exceed your customers' expectations. If you do, they'll come back over and over.
9) Control your expenses better than your competition. This is where you can always find the competitive advantage.
10) Swim upstream. Go the other way. Ignore the conventional wisdom.

After your students have had a moment to digest the list, ask them to vote on which rule is most important and which is least important. The results of the tally typically trigger a rich discussion: Why are some more important than others? Can (or should) a retailer ignore any of them? Why? Do they believe that Wal-Mart itself has followed these rules in recent years? Why or why not?

Questions for Reflection:

- How many students shop at Wal-Mart? What makes the experience better or worse than other stores?
- How can smaller retailers compete effectively with Wal-Mart?

Retailing Strategy

Purpose:
> To help students explore key elements of retailing strategy

Background:
> Most students are far more familiar than they initially think with retailing strategy. This exercise is designed to harness that knowledge and share it with the class.

Relationship to Text:
> Retailing Strategy (page 449)

Estimated Class Time:
> About 20 minutes

Preparation/Materials:
> This exercise works best with a whiteboard and a number of markers.

Exercise:
> Brainstorm with your students a quick list of retailer categories that they are familiar with. Possibilities include bookstores, convenience stores, after market shops (for customizing cars), coffee shops, pet stores, clothing boutiques, gift shops, etc. Then, divide your students into groups of 5-7 people, and ask each group to choose a retailer category. Their goals:
> - To determine the target customers
> - To decide on their three top merchandise categories
> - To sketch the layout of their store on a section of the whiteboard
> - To develop one free service to add value for customers
>
> To build involvement, you may also want to suggest that they name their store.
>
> After about 10 minutes, call time and ask the groups to present their store to the class, along with the rationale for each element. The rest of the class typically chimes in with ideas for making smart concepts even better.

Questions for Reflection:
> - Do smaller retailers typically pay attention to these elements of retailing strategy? Why or why not?
> - How could research and technology help refine retailing strategy? If so, how?

Promotional Strategy

Purpose:
> To underscore the crucial role of salespeople in retailing success

Background:
> Many students have been at both sides of the retail sales equation, and they know from firsthand experience the value of a great salesperson. This exercise is designed to highlight potential personal selling strategies for the retail environment.

Relationship to Text:
> Promotional Strategy (page 454)

Estimated Class Time:
> About 10 minutes

Preparation/Materials:
> None needed

Exercise:
> As a class, create a quick list of retail selling strategies (e.g. selling up, suggestion selling, etc.). Then, choose an articulate, self-assured volunteer—whom you know is a good sport—for a role-playing activity.
>
> The volunteer's role: He or she is a salesperson in an upscale toy store. The goal is to make sure that each customer spends as many dollars as possible, but the salesperson knows that an overly aggressive approach will alienate well-heeled customers.
>
> Your job is to play the customer. Be sure to respond to good questions or suggestions (e.g. Who are you shopping for? Would you like to get some batteries with that toy?), but back away from an aggressive approach. Modify your responses based on how the student is doing; consider throwing in some objections if he or she is too smooth, and give a couple of easy wins if he or she is struggling. And don't forget to ham it up!
>
> After the role-play, ask your students to identify additional strategies that might have made sense.

Questions for Reflection:
- Why are great retail salespeople so rare?
- How can a retailer effectively train and motivate a sales team?
- How often should a retail salesperson approach potential customers? Why? What is the downside of approaching too often?

Retail Atmospherics

Purpose:
To help your students identify the components of effective retail atmospherics

Background:
While we all respond—positively or negatively—to the atmosphere of retail stores, many students have not given thought to the elements that create that atmosphere. This exercise is designed to highlight both the importance of an effective store atmosphere, and the components that converge to create it.

Relationship to Text: Store Atmospherics (page 456)

Estimated Class Time: About 15 minutes

Preparation/Materials: None needed

Exercise:
Ask your students to identify local businesses that have standout retail atmosphere. Encourage them to consider both positive and negative examples and to be as specific as possible about what works and what doesn't. You may want to remind them that the effectiveness of retail atmosphere is highly dependent on the target audience. The retail atmosphere at *Hot Topic*, for instance, is compelling for many young people, and, uh, repelling for some of their parents (which may be part of their highly successful strategy!).

Divide your class into seven groups, and assign each group one of the topics below. Ask them to consider how they could use atmospherics to maximize the effectiveness of their venue. Encourage them to consider everything from decorations, to layout, to scent, to furnishings, to signage, to color, to music.

- Your classroom
- Your college or university campus
- Music store
- Vintage clothing store
- Office supply store
- Pancake restaurant
- Toy store

Ask each group to report their results to the class, and ask the class to provide feedback. What elements seem most effective? How important are atmospherics?

Questions for Reflection:
- How are atmospherics perceived differently across cultures? Why?
- Are great atmospherics enough for a competitive advantage? Why? (Think Victoria's Secret, Hooters, Bath and Body Works, etc.)

Vending Machines

Purpose:
> To highlight the role of vending in direct marketing

Background:
> Traditionally, vending machines in the U.S. have carried low end products like snack foods and soft drinks. However, as the text mentions, interest in vending machines for higher end products has recently surged, fueled perhaps by growing consumer comfort with direct marketing over the Internet. This exercise is designed to help students explore the potential of vending.

Relationship to Text:
> Automatic Merchandising (page 469)

Estimated Class Time:
> About 15 minutes

Preparation/Materials:
> None needed

Exercise:
> Ask your students if any of them have encountered surprising vending machines abroad. (With a little encouragement, students from Europe and Asia often offer great examples). Then, share with them that Japan, in particular, has used vending machines for a wide variety of merchandise: A few examples: bags of rice, used underwear (odd!), vegetables, short anime films, religious stickers, and beer.
>
> Divide your class into groups of 3-5 students, and give them ten minutes to develop a product that will be a vending machine hit in the US (the ideas from abroad can be a great source of inspiration). Ask them to consider packaging, pricing, promotional strategy, and location of vending machines (and you might want to remind them to keep it clean and legal!).
>
> When you call time, ask the groups to present briefly to the class, including the reasons why their product would be successful in vending machines. Encourage them to think well outside the box. The results are usually innovative and entertaining, helping the whole class to think in new directions.

Questions for Reflection:
- What are the potential downsides of automatic merchandising?
- How might technology change the vending industry in the future?

Chapter 15
Integrated Marketing Communications

NOTE: Question number four in the *Applying Concepts* section on page 516 of the text, fuels a rich class discussion regarding the change in the McDonald's promotional message. It seems to work especially well to either kick-off or wrap-up the chapter.

Understanding Integrated Marketing Communications

Purpose: To help students understand the challenge and complexity of integrated marketing communications

Background:
Effective integrated marketing communications is more complex than it initially seems to many students. This exercise is designed to help them understand both the complexity and the necessity of coordinating promotional messages in the face of overwhelming clutter.

Relationship to Text: Chapter Overview (page 482)

Estimated Class Time: About 5 minutes

Preparation/Materials: None needed

Exercise: Ask your class how many different promotional messages they have seen or heard today. (Some classes take a few moments to realize how astronomical the number really is!) Where and how did they receive those messages? What were the messages specifically? (Many students won't remember, which helps them better understand the point about clutter.)

Then guide them beyond today: What are all the potential ways that consumers can receive messages about goods and services? (Encourage them to consider *all* the possibilities...) Why is it so hard for a marketer to coordinate messages from so many sources? Probe for depth (e.g. some of the message sources—such as word of mouth—are out of the marketer's control).

After a few moments of discussion, most classes will have a clear sense of why integrated marketing communications is so necessary, yet so challenging.

Questions for Reflection:
- What are the ethical issues regarding promotional clutter? Is there likely to be consumer backlash?
- What role has the Internet played marketing communication? (You may want to emphasize that the Web has put more promotional power in the hands of consumers, which can either work for or against marketers.)

The Importance of Teamwork

Purpose:
To highlight the challenges and the potential benefits of effective teamwork

Background:
Integrated marketing communications will fail without effective teamwork. Workers and managers must coordinate across departments and even across companies to create a seamless promotional message for consumers.
This exercise is designed to give students a chance to hone their understanding of teamwork, and to develop their personal team working skills.

Relationship to Text:
Importance of Teamwork (page 485)

Estimated Class Time:
About 30 minutes

Preparation/Materials:
You'll need plenty of newspapers, and a role of masking tape for each 3-5 person group.

Exercise:
Announce that the purpose of this exercise is for each group of students to use the newspaper and tape to build the best possible tower that they can build in 15 minutes. (When they protest that they can't possibly build a tower from those materials, assure them that they'll figure it out…which they will do beautifully!)

Before you divide the class into groups, help them determine the criteria for "best" (e.g. tallest, widest, wackiest, etc.). Quickly brainstorm the possibilities, and as a class, vote on 3-5 criteria. Then, divide the class into groups of about 5 students. Earmark one student per group to be the observer, and let the building begin!

When you call time, ask the observer from each group to present the tower, and to comment on the group process. Encourage observers to cover key issues such as how (or whether) a leader emerged, how much time the group spent planning their approach, and how the group resolved conflict.

Questions for Reflection:
- How does a lack of teamwork affect integrated marketing communications? What are examples of companies that send fragmented messages?
- What are some of the outside organizations that need to understand and execute the core promotional message? (Possibilities include ad agencies, web development firms, etc.) Is it easier or harder to coordinate with these groups? Why?

Noise and the Communications Process

Purpose:
To demonstrate how poor writing interferes with good communication

Background:
Practically everyone knows that writing well is important, but examples of tortured writing help us understand just how important it can be. This quick exercise should make your students laugh, while vividly illustrating the potential impact of poor writing.

Relationship to Text:
The Communications Process—Noise (page 487)

Estimated Class Time:
About 5 minutes

Preparation/Materials:
None needed

Exercise:
Share these examples of wacky signs, allegedly spotted in public places:
- *Over the emergency exit in a small hotel*: This door is not to be used for entering or exiting the building
- *In a university faculty lounge*: At the end of the day, please empty the coffee pot and stand upside down on the draining board
- *At a conference in Las Vegas*: For anyone who has children and doesn't know it, there is a day care on the first floor
- *In the window of a dry cleaner*: Anyone leaving garments here for more than 30 days will be disposed of
- *On the ladies room in a New York office tower*: Restroom out of order. Please use floor below.
- *At the information desk of museum in Paris*: Visitors are expected to complain at the office between the hours of 9am and 11am daily.
- *Over a church door*: This is the gate of heaven. Enter ye all by this door. This door is kept locked because of the draft. (Please use side door.)

Ask your students if they have examples of their own to add to the list (typically, many do!). Then, be sure they understand the potential impact of what seem to be small mistakes. Help them see that language goofs, especially less amusing goofs, undermine the credibility of the sender and the trust of the receiver (e.g. "If you can't spell my name right, how do I know you'll get my order right?").

Questions for Reflection:
- How can a marketer best avoid communication blunders?
- What are the risks of technological tools (e.g. translators, spellcheckers)?

Guerilla Marketing

Purpose:
To raise student awareness of guerilla marketing

Background:

With intensifying competition across virtually every category, guerilla marketing has gained momentum as a technique to grab consumer attention with unconventional, often lower cost tactics. This exercise is designed to familiarize students with guerilla marketing, and to give them a chance to demonstrate their thinking by developing new guerilla tactics.

Relationship to Text:
Guerilla Marketing (page 496)

Estimated Class Time:
About 15 minutes

Preparation/Materials:
None needed

Exercise:

Discuss with your class the definition of guerilla marketing and how it differs from conventional marketing tactics. The text has several excellent examples, and you may want to throw in a few of your own (e.g. Red Bull apparently built buzz for its brand by distributing empty cans on the counters of popular pubs, or a local pizza parlor built its delivery service by placing UPS-like sticky coupons on every door in its delivery radius).

Divide your class into groups of 3-5 students, and challenge them to develop creative, compelling, non-traditional tactics to market each of the following products to 18-24 year-olds (developing the right brand name could certainly be part of the process). Depending on your class, you may want to warn them to keep it clean….

- Peanut butter
- A new kind of printer paper
- A fruit-flavored energy drink
- A digital camera
- A new candy bar
- An on-campus health clinic
- A compact car

After about ten minutes of brainstorming, assign each group one of the products to share with the class. You will likely be amazed by their creativity. Encourage the others to build on the ideas of the group that presents for each product, using the material they developed in their own groups.

Questions for Reflection:
- What are the risks of guerilla marketing? In appealing so strongly to one market segment, are you likely to alienate other potential consumers?
- What are the ethical issues to consider? (Possibilities include deception, invasion of privacy, etc.)
- Do you think that guerilla marketing will eventually become mainstream? Why or why not?

Direct Mail

Purpose:
To examine and evaluate direct mail marketing

Background:
While many consumers discard "junk mail" unopened, overall response rates are high enough that direct mail remains a critical part of many integrated marketing communications programs. This exercise is designed to help students evaluate the quality of several direct mail pieces, and to offer suggestions for creative improvement.

Relationship to Text:
Direct Mail (page 501)

Estimated Class Time:
About 15 minutes

Preparation/Materials:
A week or two before this exercise, begin collecting direct mail marketing pieces until you have enough for five pieces for each group of 3-5 students (plus a few extra). Try to gather a wide variety of pieces.

Exercise:
Help your class understand that the success of any direct mail campaign depends not only on the quality of the list, but also on the quality and creativity of the piece itself.

Then, divide your class into groups of 3-5 students, and give each team five pieces of direct mail to evaluate. Direct them to determine which elements succeed, which fail, and why. Ask them to choose their best and worst piece, and to figure out how each could be improved.

After five to ten minutes, ask each group to share their best piece and their suggestions for improvement with the class. Help them see that the best piece is not always the most complex or expensive piece, but that an innovative approach can compensate—at least to a certain extent—for a lower budget.

Questions for Reflection:
- When does direct mail make the most sense as an integrated marketing communications tactic? Why?
- How can you ensure that you are targeting the right customers with your mailing? What criteria could you use to create your list? (Possibilities include zip code, purchase history, occupation, family status, etc.)

Chapter 16
Advertising and Public Relations

Advertising Strategies

Purpose:
> To give students a chance to develop and consider advertising strategy

Background:
> Each day, advertising surrounds virtually every student, but few give much thought to advertising strategy. This exercise is designed to highlight the role of strategy, and to underscore how it connects to the advertising messages that we see each day.

Relationship to Text:
> Advertising Strategies (page 522)

Estimated Class Time:
> About 20 minutes

Preparation/Materials:
> You may want to make a copy of the scenario below for each student.

Exercise:
> After you cover the topic of advertising strategy, divide your class into groups of 5-7 people, and give each student a copy of the following scenario:
>
> *Scenario: You run a highly successful tattoo and piercing parlor in your small west coast city, but you are fairly certain that you and your key competitor have saturated your target audience of people in their teens and twenties. To grow your business, you need to reach a new market, and research has shown that men and women in their 30s (and even some in their 40s) are increasingly interested in body art...although only a small percent have actually pursued tattoos or piercing (beyond the ears). Your goal is to develop an advertising strategy to reach this audience (e.g. comparative, testimonial, interactive, etc.), and to create the core creative message.*
>
> Give the groups 10-15 minutes to plan their approach, and then ask each team to share with the class. The results can be amazing!

Questions for Reflection:
- Is advertising more effective at bringing new customers into a category, or taking customers from your competitors? Does product life cycle play a role in your response?
- What role should research play in advertising strategy? Why?

Creating Advertising

Purpose:
> To highlight the creative development process

Background:
> Developing advertising creative is one of the most fun parts of marketing, but the process involves more strategic thinking than many students realize. This exercise is designed to give students hands-on experience developing creative from a number of different angles.

Relationship to Text:
> Creating an Advertisement (page 526)

Estimated Class Time:
> About 30 minutes

Preparation/Materials:
> None needed

Exercise:
> This exercise works best without upfront discussion. Simply divide your class into groups of 3-5 people, and direct each group to choose a product—new or existing, good or service—and to develop three ads to promote that product. The first ad must use humor, the second fear, and the third logic. Their end product will be sketches of the print versions of their ads, each including a headline and a graphic. Remind them that the best ads communicate one clear reason—rational or emotional—why the consumer should purchase the product.
>
> After about 10 or 15 minutes, call time and ask each group to present their ads to the class. The results are usually interesting and almost always very funny.
>
> Follow-up discussion: Which creative approach seems most effective? Does it vary based on the product? Why? How? What are other types of appeals? Help your students understand that marketing research should play a pivotal role in choosing and developing the right creative approach for any specific product.

Questions for Reflection:
> - How can you build your personal ability to think creatively?
> - How can a company craft a creative marketing environment?

Media Selection

Purpose:
>To expose students to hands-on media planning

Background:
>Without an effective media plan, even the best creative won't do the job. This exercise is designed to give students hands-on experience with media planning, choosing both vehicles and timing.

Relationship to Text:
>Media Selection (page 530)

Estimated Class Time:
>About 20 minutes

Preparation/Materials:
>You may want to copy the scenario below for each student.

Exercise:
>Once your class understands media planning basics, divide them into groups of 5-7 students, and distribute copies of the following scenario. (While most students seem clear on the definition of alternative music, you may want to spend a moment asking them to define the genre, so that everyone can work from the same assumptions.)
>
>*Scenario: You and your colleagues have just been hired as the marketing team for an alternative music radio station that will launch in one month, targeting a core group of men and women age 18-24. The general manager has asked you to develop the "ideal" media plan for launching the station. (For this initial draft, you may ignore budget concerns). Your challenge is to develop a highly innovative, carefully targeted plan for the first six months of operation, keeping in mind that too much exposure will turn away the alternative music crowd, but too little exposure will yield too few listeners. Assume that advertising will begin two weeks before the day of the launch. Where will you advertise? How will you time your advertising?*
>
>Give the groups about 15 minutes, and then ask them to present to the class. Most teams develop radically different plans, demonstrating firsthand that media planning is more of an art than a science.

Questions for Reflection:
- Does non-traditional media (e.g. text messages) constitute an invasion of privacy? "Commercial pollution"? Why or why not?
- When a campaign uses multiple media vehicles, how can you measure the effectiveness of each individually?

Cross Promotion

Purpose:
> To highlight the growing importance of cross promotional advertising

Background:
> Cross promotions can be a cost-effective means of creating synergy between brands (e.g. family movies and fast food), helping both to grow beyond where they could on their own. This exercise is designed to highlight the importance of cross promotion by giving students the chance to explore high potential partners across a range of categories.

Relationship to Text:
> Cross Promotion (page 540)

Estimated Class Time:
> About 15 minutes

Preparation/Materials:
> None needed

Exercise:
> Divide your class into groups of 5-7 students. Write each of the following categories on the board:
> - Blue jeans
> - Pizza
> - Pick-up truck
> - Television network
> - Star athlete
> - Clothing boutique
> - Website

Direct the groups to choose one specific player in each category (e.g. Rock & Republic Jeans, or Abbots Pizza), and to choose three cross promotion partners for each. Give them about ten minutes, and then ask each group to share their ideas for one of the categories until you have covered all seven. Encourage the other groups to chime in with their additional ideas for that category at the end of each brief presentation.

Questions for Reflection:
- What are some particularly strong examples of actual cross-promotion? Why were they effective?
- What are the potential pitfalls of cross promotion?
- Which industries can particularly benefit from cross-promotion? Why?

Advertising Pretesting

Purpose:
>To demonstrate advertising pretesting

Background:

>Pretesting advertising creative not only raises the likelihood of a successful campaign, but also lowers the risk of an expensive failure, which is especially significant in the face of rising media costs. This exercise is designed to demonstrate how pretesting could work, while giving students another opportunity to develop their creativity.

Relationship to Text:
>Pretesting (page 541)

Estimated Class Time:

>About 25 minutes (NOTE: This exercise works best at the beginning of class.)

Preparation/Materials:

>Create a brief survey to rate TV ad concepts. Question 1: On a scale of 1-5, rate how much you liked the ad concept. Question 2: On a scale of 1-5, rate your likelihood of purchasing this product. Make enough copies so that students can rate each concept. Also, consider providing a stack of large, plain white paper to create storyboards.

Exercise:

>Divide your class into groups of 5-7 people and announce that each group represents an ad agency. The agencies are competing for the multi-million dollar account of a cosmetics company, which is launching a new perfume targeted toward urban men and women in their 20s. Each agency must develop a TV ad concept for the perfume—including the product name—and then create the storyboards (a series of rough pictures) for their ad. The winner will be chosen based on pretesting results.

>Before they begin, share the survey with the class. Help them decide if the winning ad should be the most likeable ad, or the one that generates the highest purchase intent.

When their concepts are complete, ask each group to present their storyboard, and explain any additional features (music, voiceovers, special effects, etc.). After each presentation, give the class a moment to complete the survey. Be sure that they write the group number at the top of each survey they complete.

Then, ask for a volunteer to tally the surveys during the remainder of the class period. The agency with the highest pretest scores wins the account. (Both small candies and extra credit points work great for prizes!)

Questions for Reflection:
- What are other important questions for pretesting?
- Is pretesting important for small companies with severely limited budgets? Why or why not?

Chapter 17
Personal Selling and Sales Promotion

Purpose:
To explore myths and facts about personal selling as a career

Background:
Although about 60% of marketing majors choose a sales position as their first job after college, personal selling retains a negative, "huckster" reputation. This quick exercise is designed to highlight how far personal selling as a career has evolved beyond the stereotype.

Relationship to Text:
The Evolution of Personal Selling (page 554)

Estimated Class Time:
About 5 minutes

Preparation/Materials:
None needed

Exercise:
Before you delve into the chapter, ask your class to share the characteristics of their ideal first job after graduation from college. As they call out their responses, you may want record them on the board. Typical answers: great salary, advancement potential, different every day, don't need to sit in a cubicle all day, independence and control, etc.

Then ask them what careers are likely to deliver these qualities. While some students have ideas, many say a career this good simply doesn't exist. This gives you a prime opportunity to introduce personal selling, which—surprisingly to many students—embodies each of the qualities listed above, plus the opportunity to develop a wide networks relationships, to solve interesting problems, and to hone communication skills, all of which can lead quite quickly to senior management positions.

Questions for Reflection:
- What are the downsides of a career in sales?
- How can you identify the "right" company for a personal selling career? What questions should you ask? Why?
- What qualities would the "right" company be seeking in their sales team?

Selling and Memory

Purpose:
> To demonstrate the connection between selling and memory

Background:
> Effective sales presentations—especially in a B2B context—must "cut through the clutter" in way that the prospect remembers (in a positive light, of course!). This exercise is designed to illustrate concepts that will help create more memorable presentations.

Relationship to Text:
> Sales Process (page 567)

Estimated Class Time:
> About 5 minutes in one class period, about 10 minutes in the next class period (and well worth the time!)

Preparation/Materials:
> Before the second class period, you'll need to make a transparency or a PowerPoint slide with the list of words below and the number of students who recalled each word in the right-most column.

Exercise*:
> Before you introduce the sales process, read the list of words below to your class at a slow, steady rate, without emphasizing any word more than any other. When you finish, ask your students to write down as many of the words as they can recall. Collect the papers after a couple of minutes.
>
> Before the next class period, create your visual aid as shown on the next page. When you present the chart to your class, cover the student recall section. Ask your students to guess which words most people recalled. They typically answer the first word, the last word, and the word related to your school…and typically they are absolutely correct!
>
> This leads to a great discussion of key sales presentation concepts. Help them see that the "primacy effect" (the tendency to remember whatever comes first) reinforces the need for a great first impression and a strong opener for any effective sales presentation. Likewise, the "recency effect" (the tendency to recall what comes last) supports the need for a strong close.
>
> The word related to your school demonstrates the impact of selective perception; people pay more attention to things that have meaning to them. From a sales presentation standpoint, this reinforces the need to sell meaningful benefits, which happens when the salesperson has focused on the needs and wants of the prospect.

Sometimes an item in the middle of the list has surprisingly high recall, which happens when the prospects have an unexpected emotional connection to a particular word. This, too, reinforces the need to know your prospect and to choose your words accordingly.

Questions for Reflection:
- What steps can you take to ensure a strong first impression?
- What are examples of strong and weak closes?
- How do the primacy and recency effects relate to selling yourself in job interviews?

Student Recall Table

Word	Number of Students Who Recalled Word
1. Twig	
2. Form	
3. Crew	
4. Rope	
5. Tool	
6. Vine	
7. Copy	
8. Pear	
9. Coat	
10. Seed	
11. Boat	
12. Wood	
13. Disk	
14. WORD RELATED TO YOUR SCHOOL (e.g. school name or location)	
15. Barn	
16. Road	
17. Tree	
18. Snow	
19. Lock	
20. Cart	
21. Sock	
22. Lamp	
23. Bell	
24. Arch	
25. Germ	

This exercise was adapted from McGinnis, John, "Using a Word List to Reinforce Selling Concepts," Great Ideas for Teaching Marketing, http://www.swlearning.com/marketing/gitm/gitm4e03-06.html, accessed 8/10/04

The Face-to-Face Sales Process

Purpose:
> To give students a chance to practice face-to-face selling

Background:
> Whether or not they realize it, many students are natural salespeople in their day-to-day lives. This exercise is designed to hone their face-to-face selling skills using situations that may be already familiar to them.

Relationship to Text:
> Sales Process—Approach, Presentation, Handling Objections, Closing (page 568 - 570)

Estimated Class Time:
> About 20-25 minutes

Preparation/Materials:
> None needed

Exercise:
> After you have covered the sales process, divide your class into pairs, and ask each pair to choose one of the following situations for a "sales" presentation:
> - Convincing your sister to lend you her truck for a ski trip with your friends
> - Convincing your teacher to give you an A, when you really deserve a B
> - Convincing your parents to send you on a spring vacation trip to Florida
> - Convincing someone you really like to go on a date with you
> - Convincing a cop not to give you a traffic ticket
>
> Give the class about ten minutes to prepare their presentations. Remind them to consider each stage of face-to-face selling, and give them license to fill in the details of their situation. Then, direct each pair to make their case to another pair (this works if they present as a team or if they choose one of the partners to do the talking). As you circulate around the room, you'll see that the results are often hilarious!
>
> Finish the exercise by choosing several volunteers (perhaps in return for some extra credit) to make their presentations to you in front of the class (and pick people who will play the role to the hilt!). Don't forget to throw in a few good objections. At the end of each presentation, ask the class to vote on whether or not they'd "buy." This can lead to a rich discussion of what works and what doesn't, including the approach, the arguments themselves, the role of non-verbal communication, handling objections, and closing.

Questions for Reflection:
> - What part of the sales process is most important? Why?
> - Which works better, a team presentation or an individual presentation? Why?

Salesperson Time Allocation

Purpose:
> To illustrate a key evaluation tool for salesperson time allocation

Background:
> Since salespeople often work quite independently, analysis of how they spend their time is a key variable in evaluating and coaching them for top performance. This exercise is designed to introduce a prevalent approach to salesperson time allocation.

Relationship to Text:
> Managing the Sales Effort (page 571)

Estimated Class Time:
> About 10 minutes

Preparation/Materials:
> You'll need to make a transparency or PowerPoint slide of the time allocation chart on the next page.

Exercise*:
> Present the time allocation chart to your students, and share the profiles of these three salespeople: there are two men and one woman; one has twelve years experience, one has seven years experience, and one has one year experience; their commission-based annual income levels are $80,000, $55,000, and $35,000. Be sure to tell them that these are "real-world" profiles based on a consulting project with a media company.
>
> After they've had a moment to absorb the information, ask them to guess which salesperson fits which profile. Be prepared for an interesting and lively discussion that elicits biases and stereotypes. Most students, for instance, assume that Salesperson #2 is the woman, because that person spends no time eating. They seldom assume that woman is the top earner.
>
> The answers are: Salesperson #1 is the female with seven years of experience and an annual salary of $80,000. Salesperson #2 is a male with twelve years of experience and an annual salary of $55,000. Salesperson #3 is a male with one year of experience and an annual salary of $35,000. You may want to point out that the highest earner spends the most with her current accounts, which seems to yield better results (with less effort) than time spent seeking brand new accounts.
>
> Wrap-up the exercise by asking them how they think salespeople *should* be spending their time. Would different allocations be more effective? Why or why not?

Questions for Reflection:
- How big a role should this type of analysis play in evaluating salespeople? Why?
- Should salespeople be evaluated beyond simply the revenue they generate each period? If so, what other evaluation tools would make sense?

Time Management Analysis Chart

Activities	Salesperson 1	Salesperson 2	Salesperson 3	Avg.
Face-to-face selling	13%	21%	33%	22.3%
Account Servicing (customer problems, questions, etc.)	21%	14%	7%	14.0%
Sales Call Planning	8%	7%	3%	6.0%
Proposal Preparation	7%	8%	4%	6.3%
Prospecting	2%	2%	6%	3.3%
Paperwork	9%	16%	1%	8.7%
Traveling	12%	14%	19%	15.0%
Waiting	2%	4%	10%	5.3%
Eating	5%	0%	5%	3.3%
Sales and Other Mtngs	8%	5%	10%	7.8%
Self-Improvement	2%	0%	1%	1.0%
Training	0%	0%	0%	0%
Copywriting	2%	4%	0%	2.0%
Cold Calling	3%	3%	0%	2.0%
Collection Calls	6%	2%	1%	3.0%
TOTAL	100%	100%	100%	100%
Hours/Day Selling	10.7	13.2	12.1	12.1

*This exercise was adapted from Hair, Joseph, "An Exercise that Makes Salesperson Time Allocation Fun and Interesting," Great Ideas for Teaching Marketing, http://www.swlearning.com/marketing/gitm/gitm25-3.html, accessed 8/4/04

Consumer Sales Promotion

Purpose:
　　To explore consumer promotion options

Background:
　　When considering consumer promotions, some students have trouble thinking beyond coupons. This activity is designed to push beyond that barrier by encouraging students to explore consumer promotion options for a range of businesses.

Relationship to Text:
　　Consumer-Oriented Sales Promotions (page 580)

Estimated Class Time:
　　About 20 minutes

Preparation/Materials:
　　None needed

Exercise:
　　Break your class into groups of 3-5 students. Challenge each group to develop a creative consumer sales promotion for the following businesses:
- Baskin-Robbins ice-cream store
- Jet Blue airline
- The Wall Street Journal
- Office Depot
- Toyota Prius
- Fanta Cola

Direct them to create one piece of consumer communication for each sales promotion idea.

Encourage your class to think outside the box, to consider using options like games, contests, sweepstakes, and sampling to create a competitive advantage. Example: A local sub sandwich shop could sponsor a sandwich of the month contest, naming the winning sandwich after the winner, and offering it on the menu for one month.

After 10-15 minutes, ask each group to share their favorite idea with the class. The results are typically excellent!

Questions for Reflection:
- Does sales promotion make more sense for some product categories than for others? Why?
- Can sales promotion ever be used to both generate short-term sales *and* build brand image? How?

Chapter 18
Price Concepts and Approaches

Introduction to Pricing

Purpose:
> To underscore the wide range of real-world pricing approaches

Background:
> Explaining pricing approaches can be somewhat dry, complicated by the real-world issue that many marketers do not actually use a strategic framework when creating prices. This exercise is designed to highlight the range of approaches in a way that hooks student attention.

Relationship to Text:
> Pricing Objectives and the Marketing Mix (page 601)

Estimated Class Time:
> About 15 minutes

Preparation/Materials:
> Bring to class (or borrow from a student) a wristwatch that looks nice and is not a well-known brand such as Timex, Rolex, or Swatch.

Exercise*:
> At the beginning of class, pass the wristwatch around the room and ask each student to write on a slip of paper the price that they would write on the price tag if they were selling this watch new in their store.
>
> Gather the papers, and ask a student to write the prices on the board as you read them aloud. The prices are sure to vary widely from unbelievably cheap to highly overpriced, and will likely include several examples of odd pricing.
>
> Ask for volunteers to share their prices and the reasons for them. Use their comments to demonstrate pricing approaches from cost-plus pricing, to odd-even pricing, to competitive pricing, to loss leader pricing, to pulling-a-price-out-of-thin-air pricing, etc. You could also use their assumptions to highlight the importance of store type and store image.

Questions for Reflection:
- Why do many marketers not use a strategic approach to pricing decisions?
- How does pricing relate to brand image? Why?

---

* Adapted from Lewellen, Bob, "The Wristwatch Approach to Pricing," *Great Ideas for Teaching Marketing*, http://www.swlearning.com/marketing/gitm/gitm08-1.html, accessed 8/10/04

115

Pricing and Market Structure

Purpose:
> To help students better understand the different categories of competition

Background:
> Identifying and understanding the competitive climate plays a critical role in smart pricing decisions. This exercise is designed to review categories of competition and to sort out potential misunderstandings, especially regarding the difference between monopolistic competition and monopolies.

Relationship to Text:
> Price Determination in Economic Theory (page 608)

Estimated Class Time:
> About 10 minutes

Preparation/Materials:
> None needed

Exercise:
> Direct students to work with the one or two people sitting next to them to brainstorm—in five minutes—a list of industries that compete in each of the four categories: pure competition, monopolistic competition, oligopoly, monopoly.
>
> After five minutes, reconvene as a class and ask your students to call out examples by category as you list them on the board. This will give you an opening to straighten out confusion among the categories. When the lists are complete, it will be clear that monopolistic competition and oligopoly are the dominant categories.
>
> Helpful discussion question: Does the type of competition tend to evolve? If so, how? Why? (Many industries seem to move from monopolistic competition to oligopoly, as major players buy out competitors in the on-going struggle to build share. Example: PCs)

Questions for Reflection:
- How does each market structure impact pricing decisions?
- How can marketers monitor changes in the competitive climate on an on-going basis?

Price Elasticity

Purpose: To demonstrate how price elasticity relates to our daily lives

Background: Often without realizing it, many students understand and apply the concepts of supply, demand, and price elasticity. This quick, discussion-based exercise is designed to demonstrate that these concepts are directly relevant to their lives, and completely consistent with their intuition and common sense.

Relationship to Text: The Concept of Elasticity in Pricing Strategy (page 609)

Estimated Class Time: 5-15 minutes (depending on whether or not your break the class into groups)

Preparation/Materials: You may want to copy the scenario and the questions below for each student.

Exercise: Ask your students how many of them drink coffee. With a little probing, you could divide them into four groups based on whether they are light (less than 1 cup per day), medium (1-2 cups per day), heavy (more than 2 cups per day), or non-coffee drinkers. (If you have less time available, this exercise also works well as a full-class discussion.) Share the scenario below, write the following questions on the board, and ask each group to try to reach a general consensus regarding their response. Direct them to appoint a spokesperson and report back to the class after about five to ten minutes. Compare and contrast responses among the groups.

Scenario: The price of coffee in all of its forms (from prepared drinks at Starbucks to whole beans at the grocery store) has suddenly doubled. What will you do? How (if at all) will your coffee-drinking habits change? What factors will influence you?

When you circulate among the groups, encourage them to consider the influence of the following factors:

- Why do they drink coffee? For the taste? To socialize? For the caffeine?
- What portion of their discretionary income do they currently spend on coffee? How would that change with the price increase?
- How would their friends/families influence them?
- Are appealing substitutes (e.g. tea, soda) easily available?
- Would timing of the price increase change their responses? (e.g. final exam week versus summer vacation?)

Questions for Reflection:
- How does the concept of price elasticity relate to pricing and revenue?
- How can you determine the elasticity of a given category?

Price Elasticity and Revenue

Purpose:
> To further explore the link between price elasticity and revenue

Background:
> Price elasticity has a dramatic impact on the success or failure of price increases, and the relationship is clear to most students. This exercise is designed to further explore that relationship and the factors that drive it, so that students can hone their planning and analysis skills.

Relationship to Text:
> Elasticity and Revenue (page 612)

Estimated Class Time:
> Less than 10 minutes

Preparation/Materials:
> None needed

Exercise*:
> Ask your students to consider what would happen to total revenue if a local bus system—which currently charges rock bottom prices—raised fares by 50%? (Your own local transportation system may provide an excellent hypothetical example.) Ask them to defend their thinking.
>
> Would their responses change long-term versus short-term? What variables would impact their answers? Encourage them to consider alternatives such as income levels in the town, the availability of alternative transportation such as carpools, the price of gasoline, the local image of public transportation, etc.
>
> Then, ask them to consider how these variables might change over time. For instance, a town could invest in urban renewal, more parking lots, or safer bike paths. The price of gasoline might change, or the town might employ tax incentives for public transportation users. Privatization is a possibility as well.
>
> Be prepared for a lively discussion, since students often disagree on the potential impact of each of these issues.

Questions for Reflection:
> - How could you get consumers "on-board" with price increases? Could (or should) PR play a role?
> - What are the ethical issues connected with price increases?

---

*This exercise was adapted from the text.

Pricing on a Global Basis

Purpose:
To explore how pricing considerations differ across international borders

Background:
Even as globalization makes the world seem smaller, prices for similar goods and services vary dramatically from country to country. This exercise is designed to explore the reasons behind the differences. It works especially well if you have international students or if at least some of your students have traveled abroad.

Relationship to Text:
Global Issues in Price Determination (page 619)

Estimated Class Time:
About 10 minutes

Preparation/Materials:
None needed

Exercise:
Ask your international students (or those who have traveled) to address the prices of the following items in other countries. Probe for information from as many places as possible and don't hesitate to include your own experience as well.
- Internet access
- Meal from McDonald's
- PDA
- Trendy blue jeans
- Toyota Corolla
- Popular CD
- Visit to the dentist
- Gallon of gasoline

Then ask them to address how the prices compare to prices for similar products in the U.S. What accounts for the differences? Encourage them to consider the full range of relevant factors, including pricing objectives, the local economies, the competitive structure of the markets, varying perceptions of value, government regulations, and national culture. The discussion is usually both interesting and rich.

Questions for Reflection:
- In the age of the Internet, is it reasonable for one company to charge different prices for the same product in different countries? Why or why not?
- Over a ten-year horizon, are the factors that lead to different prices in different countries likely to become more or less influential? Why?

Chapter 19
Pricing Strategies

The Art of Pricing

Purpose: To highlight the presence of non-mathematical factors in pricing decisions

Background: Clearly, quantitative analysis plays a key role in pricing decisions. Most successful companies use a range of mathematical formulas to help them cover both overhead and cost of goods, while meeting profitability targets. However, creativity and market knowledge also play a significant role. This exercise is designed to highlight those factors.

Relationship to Text: Pricing Strategies (page 628)

Estimated Class Time: About 20 minutes

Preparation/Materials:
You'll need to gather between seven and ten different products. Be sure to cover a range of categories, and include products purchased through a variety of distributors (e.g. retail, discount club, home parties, the Web, mail-order, etc.). Display the products on a table or desk at the front of the room. Also, prepare a small index card for each item with a brief description the its many uses and benefits.

Exercise*: Choose student "hosts" (who you know are hams) for each product, and invite them to the front of the room. Divide the rest of the class into two teams (more teams for a group of over forty students).

Then, one by one, ask the hosts to "sell" their products to the class by reading the cards. Direct each team in turn to call out their best guess regarding the price of each item. The host can respond with either "higher" or "lower" or "correct." Any team that guesses the right price within 30 seconds earns ten points. Energy and excitement build as the teams moves through the products and begin to really compete. A small prize for the winning team heats up the contest nicely.

When the game is complete, point out to your students the wide range in their guesses for each item. Encourage them to explore the reasons for the variation, which usually provides an excellent springboard for discussing the role of creative, psychological elements in determining pricing strategy.

Questions for Reflection:
- How can a marketer influence consumer perceptions about pricing?
- What role should competition play in pricing strategy?

---

*This exercise was adapted from Bulas, Laura, "Pricing...An Art or a Mathematical Formula," *Great Ideas for Teaching Marketing*, http://www.swlearning.com/marketing/gitm/gitm14-1.html, accessed 8/4/04

Pricing Strategies

Purpose:
> To underscore the pros and cons of each key pricing strategy

Background:
> The three key pricing strategies are quite different, each offering the potential for significant benefits and risks. This exercise is designed to help students understand the tradeoffs among the three approaches.

Relationship to Text:
> Pricing Strategies (page 628)

Estimated Class Time:
> About 20 minutes

Preparation/Materials:
> None needed

Exercise*:
> After you cover the pricing strategies, divide your class into three teams. Assign each team one of the three strategies, and direct them to prepare an argument for why their strategy makes sense for each of the following products:
> - Video game for teenage girls
> - Digital television
> - Fuel additive that boosts automobile mileage
> - Monitored burglar, smoke, and fire alarm
> - New brand of men's cologne
>
> After about ten minutes, ask each group to present their arguments. Then, after the three presentations for each product, ask the class to vote on which strategy makes the most sense. (This exercise works best if you request a different speaker from each group for each product.)

Questions for Discussion:
> - How could you monitor the success of your pricing strategy?
> - Would the promotional strategy be likely to differ for each pricing strategy? If so, how? Why?

---

*This exercise was adapted from the text.

Personal Pricing Strategy

Purpose:
To help students internalize the key elements of pricing strategy

Background:
Students often gain a visceral understanding of pricing when they apply the strategies to themselves and their careers. This exercise gives them an opportunity to do so, with the goal of attaining a deeper understanding of key considerations in the pricing decision.

Relationship to Text:
Pricing Strategies (page 628 - 633)

Estimated Class Time:
About 15 minutes

Preparation/Materials:
None needed

Exercise:
Help students understand that as they market themselves to employers, their salary is their price. Give them about five minutes to determine what pricing strategy each of them should follow (penetration, skimming, or competitive)? Why? Issues to consider (you may want to write these on the board):
- Who is their target market?
- How would they position their price to this market?
- What are the psychological pricing considerations?
- What are the image considerations?
- What are the promotional considerations?

As they prepare their strategies, encourage them to be creative, which could give them a significant competitive edge in a tight job market. You may also want to remind them that salaries can be more flexible than they initially seem.

Then, divide your class into pairs, and direct them to present to each other and to provide each other with constructive feedback (which often proves invaluable to those who are currently in the job market). Finally, ask for several volunteers to present their personal prices to the class along with their rationale.

Questions for Reflection:
- What should you learn about each specific prospective employer before developing your personal pricing strategy?
- Some marketing fields pay far more than others. For example, starting salaries in advertising are typically much lower than those in brand management. What accounts for the differences? What are the key trade-offs?

Penetration Pricing Strategy

Purpose:
> To explore the impact of penetration pricing

Background:
> Every student has valuable consumer-side experience with pricing strategies. This exercise is designed to harness that knowledge to help students better understand the impact and implications of penetration pricing.

Relationship to Text:
> Penetration Pricing Strategy (page 631)

Estimated Class Time:
> Less than 10 minutes

Preparation/Materials:
> None needed

Exercise:
> Ask your class if anyone has experienced walking into a store, attracted by an especially low price on a single item, only to walk out having spent far more than initially intended. (To trigger a lively discussion—and to amuse your class—you may want to start with a story of your own.)
>
> After your class has shared their stories (which are usually pretty entertaining), ask them to describe when this form of the penetration strategy is likely to succeed. When is it likely to fail? Why? What are the risks? Help them understand that if this approach is poorly implemented, it could seriously undermine the retailer's image and the consumer's trust.

Questions for Reflection:
- How much does pricing impact your choice of retailer? What are other key considerations?
- What role should the manufacturer of a product play in determining guidelines for retail pricing? Why?

Price-Quality Relationships

Purpose:
To explore the relationship between price and perceived quality

Background:
While many students believe a lower price is always better, the research is clear that most consumers have price limits—both on the high and the low end. No one wants to overpay, but no one wants poor quality either. This exercise is designed to explore the price limits for a variety of products.

Relationship to Text:
Price-Quality Relationships (page 642) NOTE: This exercise works well as an introduction to the price-quality section.

Estimated Class Time:
Less than 10 minutes

Preparation/Materials:
None needed

Exercise*:
Ask your class to divide themselves into partners, and to decide who will be A and who will be B. As they're organizing themselves, write the following products on the board:

A: DVD player, laptop computer, cell phone, leather jacket, pair of jeans
B: concert, decorative candle, digital camera, watch, athletic shoes

Then, direct the partners to ask each other these questions for each product on their list: 1) What is the highest price you would pay for a quality item? 2) What is the lowest price you would pay before you perceived that the quality of the item was be too low?

After a few moments, ask your class to call out prices for each item until you have determined the lowest and the highest price for each, which demonstrates the price limits. Which products have the largest range? Why? Which have the smallest range? Why? How can marketers use this information in establish their own pricing?

Questions for Reflection:
- In establishing the price limits for a product, would it make sense to disregard the very high and the very low ends? Why or why not?
- What role does competition play in consumer price limits?

*This exercise was adapted from the text